lonely planet

POCKET PHILADELPHIA

Ray Bartlett

Contents

Plan Your Trip 4

Top: Mummers Parade (p74)
Bottom: Philadelphia Museum of Art (p90)

Explore Philadelphia 29

Philadelphia Toolkit 145

TOP: AIMINTANG/GETTY IMAGES ©; BOTTOM: SAMUEL BORGES PHOTOGRAPHY/SHUTTERSTOCK ©

★ Top Experiences

The Journey Begins Here

Philadelphia is America's most American city, be it for the incredible wealth of art and culture, the historical buildings and sites, the melting pot of cultures, or the melting-in-your-mouth cuisines. I can travel around the world just by crossing a few streets, finding myself in an authentic Chinatown, the ritzy downtown or the colorful Gayborhood, unmissable with its rainbow crosswalks and flags. The city's got everything from wild nightlife to snooty cocktail speakeasies, writers' haunts and university sports bars. Each time I come back, I find there's more to like – and more to see.

Ray Bartlett

@kaisoradotcom

A novelist and travel writer, Ray has worked on more than 100 Lonely Planet titles, covering destinations as diverse as Guatemala, Korea, Tanzania, Indonesia, Japan, the Philippines and many parts of North America.

Swann Memorial Fountain, City Hall (p74)

THE BEST

History & Culture Experiences

Declared a World Heritage City by Unesco in 2015, Philadelphi protects its earliest days within the Independence National Historical Park, which includes Independence Hall and the iconic Liberty Bell, located in the Old City.

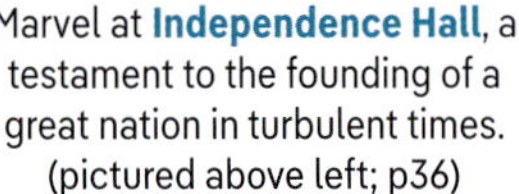

Marvel at **Independence Hall**, a testament to the founding of a great nation in turbulent times. (pictured above left; p36)

Experience interactive exhibits and live performances at the **National Constitution Center**. (pictured above right; p40)

Visit the famously cracked **Liberty Bell** that symbolizes freedom in the USA and learn about its history. (p38)

Walk down the cobblestones of adorable **Elfreth's Alley**, the oldest residential street in the country. (p33

Watch the birth of the nation brought to life at the **Museum of the American Revolution** and see the original battle tent used by George Washington. (p37)

See detailed exhibitions at the **Weitzman National Museum of American Jewish History** that illuminate the role of Jewish culture i the USA. (p40)

Right: Liberty Bell (p3

FROM LEFT: F11PHOTO/SHUTTERSTOCK ©, JANA SHEA/SHUTTERSTOCK ©, FOTOSEARCH/GETTY IMAGES

Reading Terminal Market (p58

THE BEST

Global Food Experiences

Philadelphia has an incredibly diverse food scene, a brilliant mix that runs the gamut from Burmese noodles to vegan delights

Dine in decadence at refined **Zahav**, a golden Israeli-influenced spot from award-winning chef Michael Solomonov. (p49)

Browse the **Reading Terminal Market**, where you can eat everything from Pennsylvania Dutch treats to Thai curry. (p58)

Seek out **John's Roast Pork**, a classic cash-only cheesesteak joint in business since 1930 on the city's outskirts. (p130)

Bask in elegance at **Gran Caffè L'Aquila**, with spectacular Italian food and unique, savory house-made gelatos that accompany some meals the way a salsa might. (p81)

Marvel at the stunning New American food at **a.kitchen+bar**, a James Beard semi-finalist. (p81)

Enjoy **The Love**, a bustling spot with innovative American vegetarian (and meaty) dishes, and desserts that will make you swoon. (p81)

THE BEST

Museum Experiences

Philadelphia has incredible museums that let you learn in all kinds of inventive, interesting ways. You can witness a hands-on dissection, touch incredible pieces of art, and stand back and marvel at a work in oils.

Delight in the treasure trove of one of the world's greatest impressionist art collections at the **Barnes Foundation**. (pictured above left; p94)

Delve deep into Maya mysteries and see Egyptian treasures and artifacts from around the world at the **Penn Museum**. (pictured above right; p140)

Touch all the exhibits you like at the unique, fascinating and happily hands-on **Please Touch Museum**. (p96)

Learn about dinosaurs at the **Academy of Natural Sciences** and see dioramas that bring distant worlds to life. (p95)

Explore the human heart, dissect cow eyes and dive into other sciencey stuff at the **Franklin Institute**. (p98)

Get grossed out at the collection of bizarre scientific oddities and medical curiosities, such as a skull collection and a corpse that turned to soap, at the **Mütter Museum**. (p75)

FROM LEFT: L F FILE/SHUTTERSTOCK ©, NORMAN WHARTON/ALAMY STOCK PHOTO ©

THE BEST

Public Art & Architecture Experiences

The city has a wealth of beauty that makes an urban walk worthwhile, showing off statues, murals and architecture.

Snap a selfie at the iconic cheery and cheesy red ***LOVE* sculpture** with a fountain in JFK Plaza. (p79)

Get up close to William Penn (and look up his britches!) at **City Hall**. (p74)

Marvel at the impressive **30th Street Station**, a stunning train station inside and out that's worth seeing even if you aren't traveling. (p139)

Relish the pink sandstone delight of the **Anne & Jerome Fisher Fine Arts Building**, a beautiful library in West Philadelphia with curious quips and quotes around the inside. (p139)

Admire the dragon- and flower-decorated **Chinese Friendship Gate** in Chinatown while meandering its mural-covered streets and enjoying its delicious foods. (p55)

30th Street Station (p139)

THE BEST

Bar Experiences

Philadelphia's Old City boasts the highest concentration of liquor licenses in the USA after New Orleans. Craft brewing is big, and distilling is on the rise, with several distilleries open for weekend tours and tastings.

Sip something sexy in a swanky speakeasy, such as the **Ranstead Room**, marked only by a red light on Sansom St. (p83)

Escape from Eastern State Penitentiary (or its tour, anyway) to **Bar Hygge**, which has excellent cocktails as well as great food. (p103)

Take your pick of two different bars on two different floors at **Dandelion**, where the cocktails are sublime. (pictured above right; p80)

Look out over the city from a panoramic rooftop setting like **Bok Bar**, a romantic spot to watch the sunset. (pictured above left; p133)

Shoot a game of pool at cheap and divey **El Bar**, which packs in patrons hankering for inexpensive beers and good-time karaoke sets. (p116)

Philly Pride (p150

THE BEST

LGBTIQ+ Experiences

With a delightful Gayborhood and many LGBTIQ-owned restaurants, clubs and businesses, Philly is a great place to enjoy a fabulous night on the town.

Deck yourself in rainbows for the huge **Philly Pride** festival, which takes place in June each year. (p64)

Watch a show at **Franky Bradley's**, which offers different options nearly every night of the week, from drag to stand-up comedy and rap. (p63)

Stop by **Tattooed Mom**, a fun-for-everyone LGBTIQ-owned bar. It has become a Philly institution, but more than that, it's a great place to chill out and enjoy an evening on the town. (p132)

Catch a drag show and sip drinks at legendary **Bob & Barbara's Lounge**, one of the many LGBTIQ+ spots that have become mainstream. (p82)

Shop at **Philly AIDS Thrift @ Giovanni's Room**, which calls itself the 'oldest and very best LGBTQ & feminist bookstore in the country.' (p67)

Best for Kids

Treat yourself to an afternoon of tactile pleasures at the **Please Touch Museum**, with all kinds of things to see, do, touch and experience. (p96)

Enjoy hands-on experiments, giant life-sized models and educational science and STEM-related stuff for kids to do at the **Franklin Institute**. (p98)

Appreciate the jaw size of T. rex and see life-size dinosaur skeletons, fascinating fossils and instructive dioramas at the **Academy of Natural Sciences**, a fun spot for both kiddos and parents. (p95)

See the giant crack in the **Liberty Bell** and have your kids ask rangers to tell them the history behind this iconic symbol of American liberty. (p38)

Cool off and chill out at the fountains behind the LOVE sculpture of **JFK Plaza** on a hot and humid summer day. (p79)

Best for Free

Head to the **Philadelphia Museum of Art** for its pay-what-you-want Fridays, a great way to see stunning art on the cheap. (p90)

Marvel at the ornate exterior of **City Hall** and meander around its public statues, many of which depict important founders of Philadelphia or the country's Founding Fathers. (p74)

Walk, cycle or toss a Frisbee around **Fairmount Park**, the largest city park in the USA at 2050 acres. (p95)

Wander through the cavernous halls of **Reading Terminal Market** – you don't have to buy anything to gawk at the stalls, smell the baked goods and see what's on offer. (p58)

Watch the boisterous, crazy **Mummers Parade**, a Mardi Gras–like celebration on January 1 in which fantastical floats and crazy costumes are part of the fun. (p124)

Three Perfect Days

Make the most of your visit to Philadelphia by hitting the spots in these itineraries so that you can dive right into the heart of the city.

Independence Hall (p36)

DAY ONE

Only Have One Day?

MORNING

Go early to the **Independence Visitor Center** (p36) to secure a timed ticket to visit **Independence Hall** (p36). Learn about the important principles behind the founding of the USA at the **National Constitution Center** (p40) and the **Liberty Bell Center** (p38).

AFTERNOON

Get more historical background at the **Museum of the American Revolution** (p37). Explore **Elfreth's Alley** (pictured; p33) and walk the Old City's changing waterfront, dropping into **Shane Confectionery** (p51) for some sweet treats.

EVENING

Enjoy modern Israeli food at **Zahav** (p49) (reservations required) or its sister spot **Laser Wolf** (p116) (reservations recommended) and then move on to funky **Tattooed Mom** (p132) for cocktails.

DAY TWO

A Weekend Trip

MORNING

Grab breakfast at **Reading Terminal Market** (pictured; p58) and then view the eye-popping interiors of the **Masonic Temple** (p61) or the impressive **Pennsylvania Academy of the Fine Arts** (p76).

AFTERNOON

Have lunch at **Kiddo** (p65) before or after the 12:30pm tour of **City Hall** (p74), which includes the opportunity to stand directly beneath the giant statue of William Penn. Snap a selfie in front of the ***LOVE* sculpture** (p79) in JFK Plaza.

EVENING

Get great Italian food at **Gran Caffè L'Aquila** (p81). Enjoy a craft beer at **Monk's Cafe** (p82) or see if you can track down the entrance (and a seat) at **Ranstead Room** (p83), a speakeasy with no sign.

DAY THREE

A Short Break

MORNING

Stroll or cycle through **Fairmount Park** (pictured; p95), home to several historic mansions, before dipping into the amazing collection at the **Philadelphia Museum of Art** (p90). Squeeze in the nearby **Rodin Museum** (p94) before lunch at **Sabrina's Cafe** (p100).

AFTERNOON

Spend the afternoon browsing Cezannes, Renoirs and Picassos at the **Barnes Foundation** (p154) or take a tour instead around the fascinating **Eastern State Penitentiary** (p92).

EVENING

Stretch your legs at **Rail Park** (p112). Down a pint at **Assembly Rooftop Lounge** (p103), followed by superb Middle Eastern food at **Laser Wolf** (p116). Enjoy live music at **Johnny Brenda's** (p117) or play pool and sing karaoke at **El Bar** (p116).

If You Have More Time

Explore the **South 9th Street Italian Market** (p122) and then be blown away by **Philadelphia's Magic Gardens** (p125), artist Isaiah Zagar's mosaic masterpiece, a colorful, almost psychedelic work made of found objects and glass.

Head to University City for lunch at **White Dog Cafe** (p137) and chuckle at all the dog-related knickknacks. Stroll around the UPenn campus, dropping into the **Penn Museum** (p140) and the beautiful **Anne & Jerome Fisher Fine Arts Building** (p139), taking time to see its interior as well. Check out what's showing at the **Institute of Contemporary Art** (p140).

Hit up the Gayborhood for fun times at dive bars such as **Dirty Franks** (p67), a friendly neighborhood spot with dartboards and cheap drinks. If a drag show isn't happening there, try **Franky Bradley's** (p63), another favorite. If a show isn't your style, consider a cold and frosty pour at mellow LGBTIQ-owned **Tattooed Mom** (p132).

White Dog Cafe (p142)

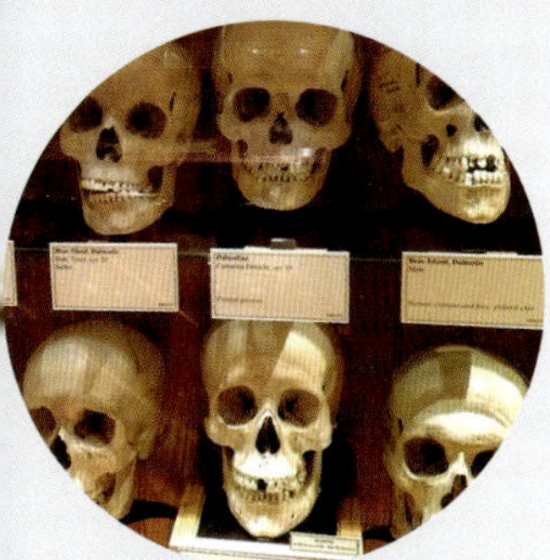

A City Day Trip

For a creepy-themed day, head to **Eastern State Penitentiary** (p92). After wandering the spooky corridors, grab a bite to eat at **Bar Hygge** (p103) or **Sabrina's Cafe** (p100) and then zip to the **Edgar Allan Poe National Historic Site** (p110).

Check out the **Mütter Museum** (pictured; p75), which has exhibits of bizarre illnesses, maladies and scientific curiosities. If you're done with the dark and ready for something cheery, head to the **Barnes Foundation** (p154) for a calming and incredible collection of impressionist artworks.

Finish the day with hand-drawn noodles in **Chinatown** (p60) or opt for a fancy sit-down spot like **Gran Caffè L'Aquila** (p81).

On a Rainy Day

Philadelphia has so much to do indoors on a rainy day that you'll barely need an umbrella. Start your day with a wander around the cavernous hall of **Reading Terminal Market** (p58) for a great breakfast.

Hop in a taxi (or use the umbrella) to get to the **Museum of the American Revolution** (pictured; p37) with its impressive audio-visual displays. Alternatively, if art is more your style, spend several hours at the **Philadelphia Museum of Art** (p90).

End the day by grabbing a quiet corner in the beautiful **Anne & Jerome Fisher Fine Arts Building** (p139) and reading a book in this exquisite learning space.

Get Prepared

BOOK AHEAD

Two months before
Book hotel reservations as soon as possible for the **Mummers Parade** (p124) and **Philly Pride** (p150). Prices increase the closer it gets to your arrival date.

Three weeks before
Reserve a table at high-end restaurants like **Gran Caffè L'Aquila** (p81).

One week before
Scan social media for the latest restaurant and bar openings, and upcoming art exhibitions.

Manners Matter

Philadelphia has a high number of people experiencing homelessness, and you'll likely see some folks on the streets. Some may ask for money or food. Whether you choose to engage with them or not, be respectful and polite. A firm 'sorry' or 'not right now' is all that's needed if you'd like to keep moving along.

Cheesesteak Etiquette

When ordering a Philly cheesesteak, it never hurts to at least sound like a local even if you're not one. Here's how to talk the talk. Specify the cheese first: American, Cheez Whiz or provolone. Then it's 'wit' (with onions) or 'wit-out' (without onions). 'One provolone, wit. One Whiz, wit-out,' gets you two cheesesteaks, one with provolone and onions, one with just Whiz cheese. Easy, right?

Things to Know

Museum opening days Most Philadelphia museums close for two days in the middle of the week, often Tuesdays and Wednesdays, so it's vital to plan your visit rather than simply showing up.

Parking tickets Philly's cops work a late beat, with some places staying patrolled until 3am on Fridays and Saturdays. Make sure to pay for the proper amount of time and park only in properly marked areas.

Happy hour Unlike some cities where happy hours are either prohibited or apply to food only, Philly proudly offers great deals on drinks and meals during those late afternoon hours. Sometimes it's two-for-one specials and other times it's a discount.

Independence Hall tickets Download the recreation.gov app to book tickets, which saves you from visiting in person but costs $1.

TIPPING

Tipping is expected in many restaurants, but at some, it's included on the bill already. You might not have the same hotel room cleaners for your whole stay, so tip daily rather than at the end of your stay.

Restaurants

Bars

Taxi & rideshare drivers

Hotel cleaning staff per day

DAILY BUDGET

Budget: Less than $150

- Dorm bed: $30
- Sightseeing/admission fees: $40
- Philly cheesesteak: $12
- Three slices of pizza: $15
- Pabst Blue Ribbon and a shot: $3.50
- PHLASH bus day ticket: $5

Midrange: $150–350

- Double room in a hotel: $150
- Lunch at a chic cafe: $30
- Guided tour: $10–30
- Dinner without alcohol: $40–60
- Show: from $25

Top End: More than $350

- Chic hotel room: $200–500
- Lunch with alcohol: $45
- Dinner with alcohol: $130–250
- Two cocktails: $50
- VIP drag show admission: $60
- Rideshare to airport: $35

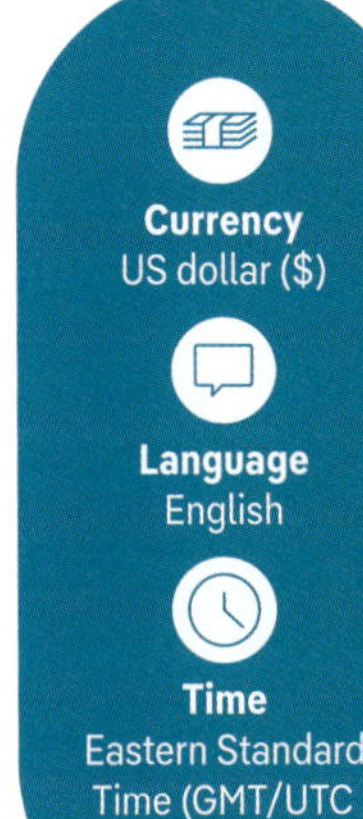

TIP

Assuming it's not cold or icy out, Philadelphia is a great cycling city, and the Indego app lets you hop on and hop off bikes all over town. Bring a helmet and ride, baby, ride.

When To Go

Philadelphia is gorgeous year-round, whether with the pink petals of blooming cherry trees or a dusting of freshly fallen snow – it's even fun in the scorching summer heat.

Philadelphia is such a popular place that you don't gain much by trying to schedule your visit around a specific season. Instead, keep certain events in mind (including those listed below) when it may be harder and more expensive to find a hotel, plus there might be crowds and road closures.

Philly is a four-season city, with a winter that typically sees a few snowfalls and even a blizzard between November and February, with a temperate, sometimes rainy spring that melts into summer from June to August.

The Big Events

January: Without a doubt, the **Mummers Parade** (p124) on New Year's Day is a top draw for its garish costumes, colorful floats and we're-going-to-party-even-if-it's-freezing-out attitude.

March: The **Philadelphia Flower Show** (p63) is unparalleled, a bonanza of blooms done up in elaborate sets, often giving visitors the sense they've stepped into a pointillist artwork where the 'paint' is the flowers themselves.

October: The **Philadelphia Film Festival** is an annual showcase of the best in independent and foreign cinema in theaters and venues across downtown Philly.

November: People come from all over the world to take part in the **Philadelphia Marathon** (p95), which also includes a half-marathon and shorter runs over

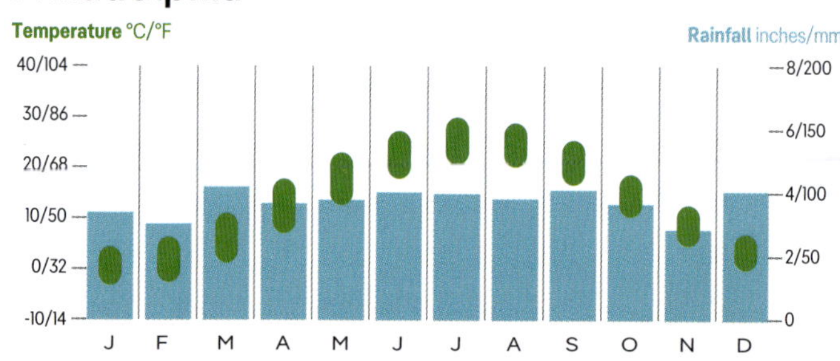

Mummers Parade (p74)

a November weekend. The route takes in the National Historic District, museums along Benjamin Franklin Pkwy and Fairmount Park.

Art & Culture

April: Gourmands drool at Philly's **Chef's Conference**, where professionals and amateurs learn new tricks of the trade, talk shop and taste up-and-coming sensations.

May: A wacky array of mobile, human-powered sculptures have to tackle a 3-mile obstacle course running through Kensington and Fishtown during the **Kensington Kinetic Sculpture Derby & Arts Festival** (p112), a fun street fest.

June: Hundreds of artists from around the country set up shop for the two-day **Manayunk Arts Festival** (p98), the region's largest outdoor juried arts festival. From jewelry and ceramics to woodwork and sculptures, pieces of all sorts are available to peruse and purchase.

September: Running since 1997, the **Fringe Festival** packs about two weeks with performance art, events, productions and creative craziness.

ACCOMMODATIONS LOWDOWN

Business hotels offer some of the best deals in town, and while they may not be as full of character as a boutique B&B, they have all the necessities. Hotels book up quickly at peak times, such as winter holidays and big Philly events.

Getting There

Visitors arrive by air at Philadelphia International Airport (PHL), by train at 30th Street Station, and by car.

From the Airport to the City Center

Train

SEPTA's Regional Rail service connects Philadelphia International Airport to the city. Trains run regularly between 5am and midnight, take about 30 minutes and cost $6.75 to Center City stations ($9.25 to other stations). Tickets can be purchased at kiosks at the stations, but only some accept cash. You cannot purchase a ticket once you're on the train. Conductors do come around and check tickets, so make sure you have one before boarding.

Taxi & Ride-Hailing apps

From the airport to Center City, taxis charge a fixed flat rate of $32 for the first person, plus $1 for each additional person. Ride-hailing apps, such as Uber and Lyft, cost about the same price. You must go to the designated area for ride services. Follow signs for Ride App/ Zone 7 after Baggage Claim.

Bus

SEPTA buses 37, 108 and 115 serve the airport, but they head to the outskirts of the metropolitan area instead of downtown. If you're headed to Center City, take the train instead.

Other Points of Entry

Greyhound Bus Terminal

Greyhound (greyhound.com), Peter Pan Bus Lines (peterpanbus.com), NJ Transit (njtransit.com) and the no-frills Chinatown Bus (chinatown-bus.org) all depart from the Greyhound Terminal downtown and arrive from East Coast destinations including New York City, DC and Boston. Flixbus (flixbus.com) is another discount carrier, but it doesn't have an office, just a drop-off and pick-up spot near I-95.

30th Street Station

Neoclassical 30th Street Station is a major hub for Amtrak train services, which connect to New York City and Chicago. The Acela high-speed line stops in Philadelphia on its way from Boston to Washington, DC..

Getting Around

Philadelphia has a mostly grid-based street layout, making it easy to walk, cycle or drive around the city. The Southeastern Pennsylvania Transportation Authority (SEPTA) system offers subway lines, trolleys and buses. Hop on two wheels using the city's Indego bike-share program to pedal around and see the sights.

Trains & Trolleys

SEPTA runs two subway lines: Broad Street Line (orange on the transit map) and Market-Frankford Line (blue). The Market-Frankford Line is also referred to as the El because it's an elevated line outside of the downtown area.

Several trolley lines (green) run underground along Market St and out to 30th St and beyond, where they emerge above ground.

SEPTA Regional Rail heads out to suburban destinations such as Norristown (on the line for Manayunk and Wissahickon) and Chestnut Hill East (on the line for Germantown).

The Port Authority Transit Corporation (PATCO) runs frequent subway trains to Camden, New Jersey. Stations in Philadelphia are 15/16th St, 11th/12th St, 9th/10th St all along Locust, and 8th St at Market St. Then it's a scenic ride across the Ben Franklin Bridge to Camden.

Bus

Market St is the main artery. Between the end of March and the

FROM LEFT: 4KCLIPS/SHUTTERSTOCK ©, KRTZ07/SHUTTERSTOCK ©

ESSENTIAL APP

The SEPTA app lets you view maps, routes and schedules, and plan your journey.

end of December, purple PHLASH buses make a loop around major tourist sites. Purchase tickets for cash (exact change only) on the bus.

Bicycle

Indego (rideindego.com), Philadelphia's bike-share system, has stations around the city. You need a US-registered credit or debit card to rent a bike for the walk-up rate of $15 for 24 hours, with unlimited 60-minute rides. To avoid paying extra, dock the bike before the hour is up and then simply check the bike again and use it for up to another 60 minutes.

The Indego30 ($20 per month) is the best deal if you plan to use the bikes often over three or more days. Good online resources for planning your cycling routes are GoPhillyGo (gophillygo.org) and Circuit Trails (circuittrails.org).

Cars, Taxis & Rideshares

Cabs, especially around Center City, are easy to hail. Uber and Lyft also operate here.

Driving isn't recommended in central Philadelphia. The traffic is heavy, parking is difficult and expensive, and regulations are strictly enforced.

Nearly all downtown hotels offer valet parking, but rates can be as much as $60 a day.

Public Transport Essentials

Fares & Tickets

To ride Philadelphia's public transport system, you can purchase a paper Quick Trip ticket, load a rechargeable SEPTA Key card, use a contactless bank card or pay with a digital wallet, such as Google Pay or Apple Pay. Getting a SEPTA Key is a good idea because it offers discounts on travel and has easy auto-reload options.

Buy the card at stations, SEPTA offices or retail outlets across the city, such as convenience stores and grocery stores. Find a map of locations at septakey.org/info/buy-load-locator.

Cash fares on all SEPTA transportation cost $2.50, plus $1 extra for transfers. Astonishingly, cash is still accepted for travel to any SEPTA location, but it's not the best use of your money.

Purchasing the reloadable SEPTA Key card gives you discounted fares of $2 per journey. You pay $4.50 for the card itself, a one-time fee, but this amount is credited toward future travel.

The One Day Convenience Pass ($6) is valid for eight trips on the bus, subway or trolley. There's also a three-day version for $15. The One Day Anywhere FleX Pass ($13) offers 10 rides on buses, rail and subways, including the Airport Line. Other pass options are at septa.org.

On the trains, conductors check your ticket, so make sure you're riding with one.

How to Pay

Tap your smart card (either a SEPTA Key or contactless payment) on the silver validators on buses and trolleys and in subway stations. Quick Trip tickets are swiped, not tapped (they are paper tickets, not smart cards). If you're paying with cash on the bus or trolley, put it into the fare box near the driver.

KEY TO THE CITY

Grab a SEPTA Key as soon as you arrive at the airport or 30th Street Station.

TICKETS

Fares are calculated based on how many zones are traversed during the ride. If you go from Zone 4 through Center City and to another Zone 4 stop on the other side, you've traversed 8 zones.

	Adult	Child
SEPTA	$2	Free
PHLASH	$5	$5, or $12 for Family Pass (two adults and two children)

TICKET ZONES

CC: Center City stations

Zone 1: Near Center City

Zone 2: Nearby suburbs

Zone 3: Outskirts

Zone 4: Philadelphia International Airport

A Few Surprises

Public art, quirky gems and an iconic sandwich: look closely and you'll find some great surprises in Philly.

Philly's Public Art

It's easy to spot public art in Philadelphia, but did you know that this city has more public art than anywhere else in the USA? More than 1000 murals grace walls throughout the city, turning the streets into an ever-changing art gallery. From the ***LOVE* sculpture** (p79) in JFK Plaza and ***Rocky*** (p94) to **Ben Franklin** (p38) and **William Penn** (p74), impressive pieces are everywhere.

Be There & Be Square

Many newcomers to Philly assume that the five public squares originally planned by William Penn were set in stone from day one, but in fact, for more than a century, they were fallow, almost forgotten places because nobody had decided how to pay for their upkeep and maintenance.

The squares weren't even given names initially and were simply known by their locations: Southeast, Southwest, Northeast and Northwest. Only later were they renamed after famous founding figures: **George Washington** (p46), **David Rittenhouse** (p78), **James Logan** (p97) and **Benjamin Franklin** (p32). The fifth park is where **City Hall** (p74) stands.

Now That's A Mouthful

A good-natured rivalry exists between Philadelphia and the rest of the world in the race to own the title of 'world's longest Philly cheesesteak.'

Naturally, the coveted honor should rest in Philly's hands, but in 2023, Idaho tore away the title with a 722ft-long American wit.

OFFBEAT PHILADELPHIA

Enjoy the flamboyant, wild and wacky floats and costumes during the **Mummers Parade** (p124).

Explore the creepy and fascinating interior of one of the most feared prisons at **Eastern State Penitentiary** (p92).

Look at medical oddities and get grossed out at the **Mütter Museum** (p75).

Crawl inside a giant heart or dissect cow's eyes at the **Franklin Institute** (p98).

Eastern State Penitentiary (p92)

Franklin Institute (p98)

Explore Philadelphia

Philadelphia's Walking & Cycling Tours

Philadelphia skyline
JON LOVETTE/GETTY IMAGES ©

See p48
for eating,
drinking and
shopping
listings

Explore Old City & Society Hill

If there's one place where visitors can find traces of the United States' Founding Fathers today, it's Philadelphia's Old City. A large L-shaped chunk of this neighborhood is Independence National Historical Park, where Washington, Jefferson and Franklin, et al. crafted a grand political experiment. Stroll along cobblestone streets lined with iconic landmarks, such as Independence Hall and the Liberty Bell, and immerse yourself in the birthplace of US democracy.

If history tires, this neighborhood has lots more to see. Across the sunken Delaware Expwy (I-95), old wharves have been transformed into the parks and skating rinks of Penn's Landing. South of Walnut St, largely residential Society Hill is one of Philadelphia's most stylish neighborhoods.

Getting Around

Bus
Use SEPTA buses or catch the PHLASH bus along Market and Walnut Sts.

Ferry
From late May to early September, the RiverLink Ferry shuttles between Penn's Landing and Camden's waterfront every 30 minutes.

Subway
Hop on or off the Market-Frankford Line subway at 5th or 2nd St stations.

Bicycle
Download the Indego app (rideindego.com) to rent and ride an electric-assisted bicycle. You can rent at one kiosk and return at another.

Independence Hall (p36)

THE BEST

See where the Declaration of Independence and US Constitution were signed at **INDEPENDENCE HALL** (p36).

Visit **FRANKLIN COURT**, Benjamin Franklin's former home and printing business (p39).

Be immersed in the fight for independence at the **MUSEUM OF THE AMERICAN REVOLUTION** (p37).

Witness the famous cracked bell at **LIBERTY BELL CENTER** (p38).

WALKING TOUR

Walk the Old City

Although it's dominated by Independence National Historical Park, the Old City isn't only about the events that happened centuries ago. This neighborhood also has quirky museums and relaxing parks. Set off on this walk beside the Delaware River to see what's happening in the area.

START	END	LENGTH
Museum for Art in Wood	Spruce Street Harbor Park	1.25 miles, 1 hour

1 Wooden Wonders

Prepare to be awed by what might otherwise seem uninspiring: wood. Incredible lathe-turned bowls, marquetry, nature photography and timber sculptures await you at the **Museum for Art in Wood**. The gallery puts on several exhibitions a year. Its museum collection has more than 1000 objects, and the shop sells handcrafted pieces. You can even try your hand at crafting a piece.

2 Fighting Fires

Swing by the **Fireman's Hall Museum** to peek at antique fire engines, see the tools and equipment that firefighters have used over the years and look inside an old brick building that was once the area's firehouse.

3 Atmospheric Alley

Lined with brightly painted brick row houses fluttering with flags, photogenic cobblestone **Elfreth's Alley** dates from the 1720s, making it the oldest residential street in the USA. Exploring its narrow courtyards is like stepping back in time.

4 A New Lease of Life

After sitting abandoned for decades, the early 20th-century municipal **Cherry Street Pier** has been revamped as a mixed-use public space with a pop-up market, gardens, events and artists' studios. Converted shipping containers make up the studios and food stalls, making it a perfect lunch stop.

5 Pause at Penn's Landing

Estimated to be completed in 2028, Penn's Landing is a park that's set to be filled with trees, gardens, an ice-skating rink and grassy hills. For now, you'll just have to hustle past the bulldozers and jackhammers and use your imagination.

6 Aye Aye, Captain

The **Independence Seaport Museum** offers a comprehensive range of maritime-related exhibits and interactive displays. Check out the massive ship carpenter's screwdriver, which is sure to change your views about what a simple tool can be. Some tickets include the 1944 submarine USS *Becuna* and the distinguished 1892 USS *Olympia* moored alongside the main building.

7 Put It in Park

The summer-season **Spruce Street Harbor Park** is a great place to hang out by the river in the warmer months. Relax in a two-person hammock, play free games such as ping-pong and shuffleboard, or knock back craft beers and local eats from the many stalls.

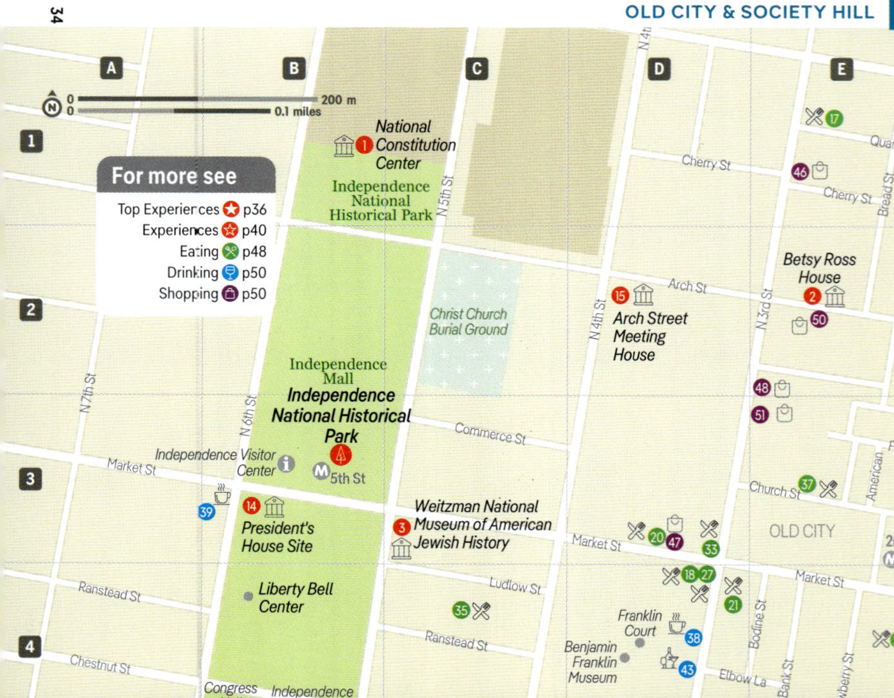
For more see
Top Experiences p36
Experiences p40
Eating p48
Drinking p50
Shopping p50
200 m
0.1 miles
National Constitution Center
Independence National Historical Park
Christ Church Burial Ground
Arch Street Meeting House
Betsy Ross House
Independence Mall
Independence National Historical Park
Independence Visitor Center
5th St
President's House Site
Weitzman National Museum of American Jewish History
Liberty Bell Center
Congress Hall
Franklin Court
Benjamin Franklin Museum
OLD CITY
2nd St
N Front St
Quarry St
Cherry St
Bread St
Elfreth's Alley
Arch St
N 3rd St
N 4th St
N 5th St
N 6th St
N 7th St
N 2nd St
Cuthbert St
Filbert St
American
Church St
Commerce St
Market St
Ludlow St
Ranstead St
Chestnut St
Bodine St
Bank St
Elbow La
Letitia St
Black Horse Alley

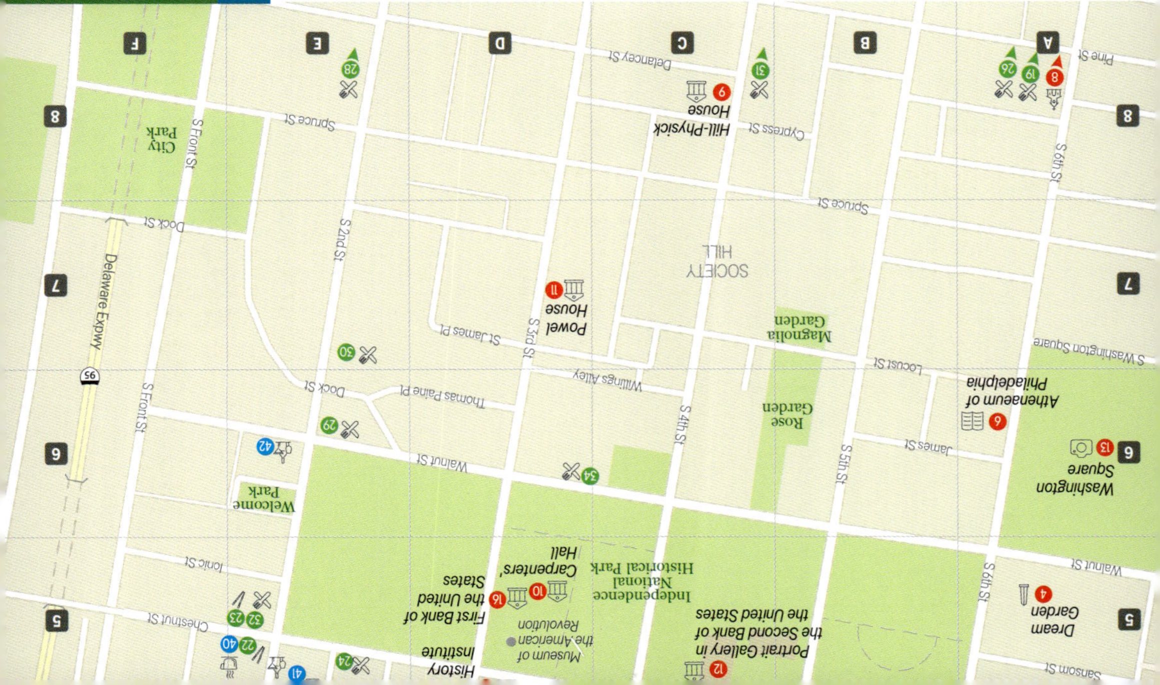

A B C D E F
5 6 7 8

Portrait Gallery in the Second Bank of the United States 12
Museum of the American Revolution
History Institute
First Bank of the United States 16
Carpenters' Hall 10
Independence National Historical Park
Powel House 11
Hill-Physick House 9
Athenaeum of Philadelphia 6
Washington Square 13
Dream Garden 4
Welcome Park
City Park
Rose Garden
Magnolia Garden
SOCIETY HILL
Delaware Expwy
95
Sansom St
Walnut St
Chestnut St
Ionic St
Dock St
Spruce St
Pine St
Delancey St
Cypress St
Locust St
James St
S Washington Square
Willings Alley
Thomas Paine Pl
St James Pl
S Front St
S 2nd St
S 3rd St
S 4th St
S 5th St
S 6th St
8 19 26 28 31 30 29 34 42 24 41 22 40 32 23

★ TOP EXPERIENCE

Independence National Historical Park

Independence National Historical Park is a stunning, almost overwhelming collection of museums, exhibits and historic buildings that keeps alive the most important event in the history of the United States: its founding. Set aside a couple of days to see everything.

MAP P34 **B3**

PLANNING TIP
The museums allow strollers, so don't worry if you're visiting with kids. If you need a wheelchair, loaners are available at the **Independence Visitor Center**.

Scan code for opening hours for the individual sites within the park.

Independence Hall

The most unmissable place at the free-to-visit Independence National Historical Park is **Independence Hall**, where the Declaration of Independence was signed and the US Constitution was written, documents that enshrined the concept of democratic rule in the United States. Entry to this World Heritage Site, a Georgian building that also served as the Pennsylvania State House, is by tour only. Inside, you'll visit the **Supreme Court Chamber**, which has been restored to look much as it did in those hallowed days of the country's founding.

Across the hall is the **Assembly Room**, with its photogenic green felt tabletops and hardwood chairs, where most of the building's notable events took place. The Declaration of Independence was approved here on July 4, 1776. George Washington sat in the chair in the center, and Abraham Lincoln's body lay here in state for two days following his assassination in 1865.

ROSEMARIE MOSTELLER/SHUTTERSTOCK ©

Museum of the American Revolution

Enter this impressive, multimedia-rich museum and virtually 'participate' in the American Revolution through interactive dioramas and 3D experiences that take you from contentment with British rule to the eventual rejection of it. Learn about the events, people, cultures and religions that participated in one of the world's most important events. Lots of hands-on displays and video stories mean kids will have as much fun as adults.

All entry tickets are timed; reserve them early online (amrevmuseum.org). A prime attraction is George Washington's battle tent, dramatically revealed after you watch a presentation about it. Actors dramatize period scenes as well, though the schedule and times vary. Check the website for details.

QUICK BREAK
Menagerie Coffee, an attractive, chilled cafe, serves single-origin coffee, snacks, pastries and sandwiches. Rough brick walls and hardwood floors give it a good ambiance.

STORYTELLING BENCHES

Between the end of May and early September, look for the 13 **Storytelling Benches** dotted around the Old City. At these spots, professional storytellers enchant listeners with tales about historical figures and events. Kids can collect a flag and a star from every storyteller on their journey, and a full set qualifies for a free carousel ride at Franklin Sq.

Liberty Bell Center

Originally called the State House Bell, the Liberty Bell was made in 1751 to commemorate the 50th anniversary of Pennsylvania's constitution. Mounted in Independence Hall, it tolled on the first public reading of the Declaration of Independence. The crack developed in the 19th century. The bell was retired in 1846 and now sits as the star attraction of the **Liberty Bell Center** (pictured).

Congress Hall

Near Independence Hall, **Congress Hall** served as the seat of the United States Congress from 1790 to 1800. It's where George Washington was inaugurated for his second term as president and John Adams took the oath of office as the nation's second president.

Benjamin Franklin Museum

The **Benjamin Franklin Museum** features a diverse collection of exhibits and artifacts related to his life and achievements. Explore interactive displays showcasing Franklin's inventions, scientific experiments and writings, including his famous Poor Richard's Almanack and contributions to the field of electricity.

The exhibition, divided into five areas that focus on one of Franklin's traits, is cleverly laid out with interactive elements and plenty of famous quotations. In the courtyard, park rangers demonstrate the printing process Franklin would have used.

MSPHOTOGRAPHIC/SHUTTERSTOCK ©

Franklin Court

The peaceful **Franklin Court**, accessible from Market and Chestnut Sts, is where Benjamin Franklin's home once stood. The house was demolished in 1812, but you can still get a good impression of its dimensions from the tubular steel 3D outline of the building designed by the architectural firm Venturi, Rauch and Scott Brown in 1976.

JUNIOR RANGER CARDS

Kids can collect NPS Junior Ranger cards as they tour the museums and exhibits. Each card has a historical figure or event and information on the back.

EXPERIENCES

Discover World-Changing Documents at the National Constitution Center

MUSEUM

MAP: 1 P34 B1

The **National Constitution Center** (constitutioncenter.org, adult/child $19/15) brings to life the potentially dry and dense US Constitution, starting with a dramatic theater-in-the-round presentation by a single actor explaining the evolution of the political experiment.

'The Story of We the People' exhibit narrates a captivating journey through the US Constitution. Interactive displays and multimedia presentations dive into detail about the founding document, from the Constitutional Convention of 1787 to contemporary debates. Temporary exhibits, covering topics like Founding Father Alexander Hamilton or the challenges of Prohibition, invite visitors to grapple with modern and historical issues through the lens of constitutional principles, fostering a deeper understanding of citizenship.

Wander the halls and be reminded of the enduring power of this radical project. In the shadow of Independence Hall (p36), the National Constitution Center stands as a pilgrimage site for those who seek to understand democracy's roots and the challenges ahead.

Meet the Famous Flagmaker at the Betsy Ross House

MUSEUM

MAP: 2 P34 E2

Nestled along cobblestone pathways, the **Betsy Ross House** (historicphiladelphia.org, adult/child $10/8) tells the story of one of the country's most enduring symbols: the Stars and Stripes, the first US flag. You get to meet 'Betsy Ross' herself (an actress in period clothing who stays in character); she's the prime attraction and a fun experience for visitors with kids. Ask her questions and watch her work on a flag while learning about the history of this icon. The modest rooms and cozy quarters offer a glimpse into the daily life of a Revolutionary-era upholsterer.

Most historians doubt that this house is actually where the first flag was made, and it's pretty certain that the house Ross lived in was next to this one. Even so, the Betsy Ross House is a highly popular tourist stop.

Get Cultured at the Weitzman National Museum of American Jewish History

MUSEUM

MAP: 3 P34 C3

The excellent **Weitzman National Museum of American Jewish History** (theweitzman.org) provides a solid introduction to the history and role of Jewish culture in the USA, covering topics from ntertainment to the Civil Rights novement. Look for the 8ft-tall heery yellow OY/YO sculpture outside that marks the start of a ascinating journey through the American Jewish experience.

Covering four floors, exhibits ange from multimedia displays to ntriguing items such as rving Berlin's piano, a Yiddish ypewriter and covered wagons used by Jewish settlers in the 800s. The ground-floor gift hop is a good spot to pick up ontemporary and traditional udaica, including books and decorative religious items such as menorah.

While the experience is specific o Jewish history, don't overlook t just because you're not Jewish: t's an eye-opening museum for visitors of any background. Many of the hurdles Jews have faced n the United States centered on mmigration, acceptance and acism: the same struggles that new arrivals continue to face.

Admire the Tiffany Glass *Dream Garden* PUBLIC ART

MAP: 4 P34 **A5**

Step from the urban into the pastoral in the east lobby of the Curtis Center. **Dream Garden** is a free-to-see luminous wall-size Tiffany mosaic made of more than 100,000 pieces of glass that depict a lush landscape. Maxfield Parrish designed this masterpiece in 1916, and it's one of only three such works undertaken by Tiffany Studios. The piece is made of 24 panels that took six months to install.

Should the beautiful glass landscape have you waxing musical, sit down at the grand piano in the building lobby that is free for visitors to play.

Put On Your Thinking Cap at the Science History Institute MUSEUM

MAP: 5 P34 **D5**

The **Science History Institute** (sciencehistory.org, free) is a must-stop for scientists and young explorers. Step into this museum's

HOP OVER TO CAMDEN, NEW JERSEY

Camden – directly across the Delaware River from Penn's Landing – has attractions, a pleasant waterside park and great views. Battleship New Jersey, the most decorated such vessel in the USA, has a 1½-hour guided tour on Saturdays and Sundays at 11am – you can even crawl in a 16in gun turret. With more than 8500 aquatic creatures from sea turtles to zebra sharks, Adventure Aquarium is one of the country's largest. As well as a fish, you can also see a pair of 3000lb Nile hippos, Button and Genny, plus a flock of African penguins in their own outdoor park.

hallowed halls to discover a treasure trove of artifacts, archives and exhibitions that offer a window into the minds of the world's greatest innovators and thinkers.

The institute's collections span centuries and continents, from rare manuscripts and laboratory equipment to chemical samples and scientific instruments. Among the relics of the past, you can trace the evolution of scientific thought and explore the interconnectedness of ideas across cultures and disciplines from ancient alchemy to modern chemistry. Learn about everything from how crayons get their colors to measuring the chemical composition of things in space.

See International Artifacts at the Athenaeum of Philadelphia LIBRARY

MAP: 6 P34 **A6**

Free exhibitions take place at the **Athenaeum of Philadelphia** (philaathenaeum.org), a special collections library occupying a National Historic Landmark brownstone building designed in 1845. Step into the Athenaeum's elegant halls to peruse rare books, manuscripts, and architectural drawings and see works of art.

The Athenaeum's extensive collection spans centuries and encompasses a range of subjects, from literature and history to science and the arts. Curiously, also on display is Napoleon Bonaparte's death mask, part of a collection of pieces donated to the Athenaeum by Joseph Bonaparte, Napoleon's elder brother and the former king of Spain, who lived in Philadelphia for a while. Book signings, author lectures and other literary events are some of the many reasons to visit.

Be Wowed by the Benjamin Franklin Bridge BRIDG

MAP: 7 P34 **F1**

For breathtaking views of Philadelphia and the Delaware River, walk or cycle across the 1.8-mile, 800,000-ton **Benjamin Franklin**

THE SUFFERINGS OF SUFFRAGE

Suffrage, the right to vote, is at the core of US democracy. The idealistic language of the Declaration of Independence is inspiring to read, but it ironically applied only to a small segment of the population when it was written: wealthy, landowning white men. Enslaved people, women, minorities, Native people and non-landowners were not allowed to participate in this grand political experiment. Voting wouldn't be legal for these groups for centuries, and in some ways, the nation is still grappling with the problems of a country where people are legally equal but often not treated as such.

Benjamin Franklin Bridge

Bridge, the longest suspension bridge in the world when it was completed in 1926. Designed by Paul Cret, the bridge connects Philadelphia with Camden, New Jersey, and it carries cars, trains, cyclists and pedestrians. It is most striking when illuminated at night.

Whether you're strolling across the bridge, admiring its grandeur from afar or simply pausing on it to take in the view, the Benjamin Franklin Bridge offers a rewarding vista. Note that the elevated pedestrian walkways close during severe weather (or even if snow is in the forecast). Only one side of the bridge is open at a time for pedestrian use.

Visit the Birthplace of the African Methodist Episcopal Church

CHURCH

MAP: 8 P34 A8

Mother Bethel AME Church (motherbethel.org, free) is the oldest piece of real estate continually owned by Black people in the USA and the first church to be founded based on racial identity, rather than solely on religious conviction, making it a defining voice in Black American identity.

The present church, the fourth on the site, dates from 1889 and features gargoyles on its bell tower. The main chapel on the 2nd floor has beautiful stained-glass windows and magnificent woodwork.

Richard Allen and Absalom Jones, formerly enslaved Black men, founded the original church in 1787. Benjamin Rush, a signer of the Declaration of Independence and among the first white revolutionaries to speak out against slavery, was an initial supporter. The church later became a stop on the Underground Railroad when Pastor Allen (entombed in the church) hid hundreds of fugitive enslaved people before the Civil War. The adjacent **Richard Allen Museum** provides further insight into the church's legacy, showcasing artifacts, documents and artwork that celebrate the contributions of Black people to religion, culture and social justice.

Meditate on Medicine at the Hill-Physick House

MUSEUM

MAP: 9 P34 C8

Once home to the 'Father of American Surgery,' Philip Syng Physick, the stately **Hill-Physick House** (philalandmarks.org, guided tour $10) has been well preserved. Physick is credited with inventing the stomach pump, as well as introducing soda to the USA. Details of his life are documented throughout the furnished rooms. Look for the toe-curling illustrations of lithotomy (an operation to remove gallstones) and the eye-watering implements used for the procedure. You're sure to leave with a renewed appreciation for modern medicine.

Visits are by tour, which take place on the hour from 11am to 3pm on Thursdays to Saturdays and from noon to 3pm on Sundays from April to November. Tours run on weekends only in March and December.

Enjoy Historic Handiwork at Carpenters' Hall

HISTORIC BUILDING

MAP: 10 P34 D5

Erected in 1774 as a calling card for the skillful work of the Carpenters' Company of Philadelphia, **Carpenters' Hall** (carpentershall.org, free) is where the First Continental Congress met and where many

YELLOW FEVER EPIDEMIC OF 1793

Soon after the euphoria of the birth of a new nation, the terrifying scourge of yellow fever hit Philadelphia. At the time, the outbreak had no known cause, and wild theories ranged from fumes of rotting waste to human-to-human contact. Cures, all ineffectual, were equally wild and included ingesting mercury and bloodletting. The knowledge that it was caused by the insidious mosquito was more than a century away. Even upstanding citizens such as Samuel Powel died, one among the 50,000 who lost their lives in the epidemic. Close to 10% of Philadelphia's residents died in less than five months.

DON'T FEED THE WILDLIFE

Some of the most entertaining moments of your visit to Philadelphia aren't inside the monuments but on the lawns and in the gardens in front of them. A host of cute furred and feathered friends makes walking around a delight. Though it's tempting to toss breadcrumbs to the squirrels and pigeons, it's healthier for everyone if you don't. Leftovers pollute and allow other less desirable vermin, such as rats, ants and hornets, to thrive, making it easier for diseases to spread. Resist that cute furry face that's begging and take a photo instead.

of the plans were discussed that would bring about the Revolution.

Despite it being part of Independence National Historical Park (p36), the local carpenters' guild still owns the building. Inside, find a plethora of exhibits and information and an intricate diorama of the hall's construction, with meticulously recreated miniature wooden scaffolding. The tile floors and stately grandeur are breathtaking.

Travel Back in Time at Powel House

HISTORIC BUILDING

MAP: 11 P34 **D7**

Stepping into **Powel House** (philalandmarks.org, guided tour $10), an elegant Georgian brick mansion, is like whisking yourself back to the 1700s. The lavish interior is spectacular, with ornate mirrors, chandeliers, gleaming wood floors and portraits that seem almost lifelike. The rooms have been meticulously restored, though they are not original.

The building was home to Samuel Powel, a mayor of Philadelphia in the colonial era, and thus a focal point of the city's social life in the 18th century. It hosted many noteworthy guests and was known for its decadence while many were struggling. Parts of the original interior are in the **Philadelphia Museum of Art** (p90).

Visits are by tour only, on the hour from 11am to 3pm, Thursdays to Saturdays and from noon to 3pm on Sundays, April to November. Tours run on weekends only in March and December.

Check Out Paintings Inside the Second Bank of the United States

MUSEUM

MAP: 12 P34 **C5**

Modeled after the Greek Parthenon, the **Second Bank of the United States** is an 1824 marble-faced Greek Revival masterpiece that now houses a free-to-visit portrait gallery (nps.gov/inde). It served as the nation's second bank until it was vetoed by President Andrew Jackson, a staunch opponent of central banking.

Today, it's beautiful inside and out. Charles Willson Peale, the top portrait artist at the time of the American Revolution, painted

Tomb of the Unknown Soldier

many of the impressive works. His depiction of George Washington is particularly popular and remains a highlight for many visitors.

Relax & Reflect in Washington Square

SQUARE

MAP: 13 P34 **A6**

On the northwest edge of Society Hill, the attractive tree-planted **Washington Square** dates from William Penn's original city plan, then called Southeast Square and used as a burial ground and pasture. The name was changed in honor of George Washington in 1825 and converted into a formal park. Today, it is officially part of Independence National Historical Park (p36).

Stop at the **Tomb of the Unknown Soldier**, erected in 1954, the only monument in the USA to the unknown American and British dead of the Revolutionary War. The marble sarcophagus and tranquil garden offer a place of reflection. Inscribed with 'Freedom is a light for which many men have died in darkness,' the tomb stands as a reminder of valor and sacrifice.

Learn About Enslaved People at the President's House Site

HISTORIC SITE

MAP: 14 P34 **B3**

The free outdoor exhibition at the **President's House Site** (nps.gov/inde) is constructed where George

Washington and John Adams had their presidential offices. Partially built redbrick walls mark the outlines of where the building once stood and frame a series of exhibits and archaeological remains that offer a window into the lives of the enslaved people who lived and worked here.

Interpretive panels and multimedia displays provide insight into their experiences, struggles and contributions to US history. The site serves as a poignant reminder of the contradictions inherent in the nation's founding principles, juxtaposing the ideals of liberty and equality with the stark realities of slavery and oppression.

Understand Quakerism at the Arch Street Meeting House

HISTORIC BUILDING

MAP: 15 P34 D2

The historic 1804 **Arch Street Meeting House** (historicasmh.org, suggested donation adult/child $5/2) is one of the oldest surviving Quaker meetinghouses in the United States. The brick wall surrounding the site is even older, built in 1728 to protect the graveyard. Today, the meetinghouse is popular for its beautiful Georgian architecture.

Start by appreciating the simplicity and elegance of the building from the outside, which reflects the Quaker values of humility and equality. Inside, tours provide insight into its history, architecture and the Quaker faith. The Arch Street Meeting House plays host to various community events, lectures, discussions and programs throughout the year. These events often focus on topics related to Quakerism, history, social justice and community engagement.

Stop By the First Bank of the United States

HISTORIC BUILDING

MAP: 16 P34 D5

The US dollar wasn't always the paragon of trade it is today, and at the time of the Revolution, many colonies printed their own currencies. Alexander Hamilton, the first Secretary of the Treasury, changed that, creating the **First Bank of the United States** (nps.gov/inde), which had the power to issue banknotes and thus established a national currency. First Bank notes were the only ones accepted when paying federal taxes, which the First Bank also collected.

The building is closed to the public, but it's impossible to ignore the 1797 building's grand neoclassical architecture. It's a popular backdrop for wedding photos. Note that the pediment carved from local teak is weathering far better than the blue marble columns that hold it aloft. The giant eagle atop the pediment is carved of mahogany and is the oldest reference to the country's national bird.

LISTINGS

Best Places for...

$ Budget $$ Midrange $$$ Top End

Eating

Breakfast & Brunch

Cafe Ole $$

17 E1
The sunshine-yellow decor makes the great muffins, pastries and sandwiches taste even better. Great coffees, lattes and teas as well. *8am-6pm*

High Street Philadelphia $$
18 D4
Many Philadelphians swear by High Street's delicious house-made breads and will come here for those alone. This spot certainly has a creative way with a breakfast or lunch sandwich. *11am-3pm & 5-9pm Tue-Thu, to 9:30pm Fri, 10am-3pm & 5-9:30pm Sat, 10am-3pm Sun*

Lombard Cafe $
19 A8
A clean, wood-floored spot that likes its mirrors, the Lombard is a fine spot for breakfast or brunch bites, as well as coffee and tea, close to the Mother Bethel AME Church. *8am-5pm*

3J's Cafe $
20 D3
Known for its excellent mochas and hot chocolates, this sweet spot has good benedicts and other breakfast plates as well. *8am-3pm Tue-Sun*

Around the World

Las Bugambilias $$
21 D4
Hefty portions of modern Mexican and Mexican-American fare served alongside colorful decor and popular margaritas. *3-9pm Mon-Wed, from 10am Thu, 10am-10pm Fri & Sat, to 9pm Sun*

Han Dynasty $$
22 E5
Szechuan cuisine in a glamorous setting that once was a bank. Pick from a variety of soups, noodles and spicy entrees. *noon-9:30pm Mon-Wed, to 11pm Thu, noon-midnight Fri & Sat, to 11pm Sun*

Buk Chon $$

23 E5
Sate yourself with Korean comfort foods, such as *jjigae* (stew) and *kalbi* (beef ribs). Dining here feels as if you've stepped into Korea for just a little bit. *11:30am-10pm Sun-Thu, to 11pm Fri & Sat*

Vegan & Vegetarian

European Republic $
24 E5
European-inspired wraps, dishes and fries (the specialty), with a rainbow of dipping sauces. It's a casual place despite a modern vibe, with lots of veggie-only options. *11am-9:30pm Mon-Sat*

Cuba Libre $$
25 E4
Vibrant Latin decor, flavorful Cuban cuisine – including several vegetarian options – and a lively atmosphere with Latin music make this spot shine. *4-9pm Mon-Thu, to 9:30pm Fri, noon-9:30pm Sat, to 9pm Sun*

Dottie's Donuts $

26 A8

Vegans rejoice. Dottie's has arrived with all the doughnuts you could want and lots of interesting daily specials in a guilt-free space where even the 'cream' is plant-based. *8am-3pm*

Fine Dining

Fork $$$

27 D4

Seasonal, locally sourced ingredients are crafted into innovative dishes with a sophisticated atmosphere and excellent service. *11am-3:30pm & 5-9pm Tue-Sun*

Twisted Tail $$$

 E8

Traditional Southern-inspired cuisine with a modern twist, plus live blues music, craft cocktails and a lively atmosphere in a historic building. *4-10pm Sun-Thu, to midnight Fri, 11am-midnight Sat, 10am-10pm Sun*

Positano Coast by Aldo Lamberti $$$

29 E6

Mediterranean-inspired seafood, handmade pasta and specialty cocktails served in a chic, coastal-feeling setting. *11:30am-9pm Tue-Sun*

Middle Eastern

Zahav $$$

 E7

Acclaimed modern Israeli cuisine featuring wood-fired dishes, mezze plates and innovative flavors served in a sleek and stylish space. *5-9:30pm Tue-Sat*

Marrakesh $$

 C8

The authentic Moroccan cuisine and traditional North African decor of plush carpets, cushions and low tables aim to transport the diner, and they certainly do. *5:30-11pm*

Malooga $$

 E5

Delicious Yemeni food is the draw, with additional Mediterranean cuisine items in a relaxed ambiance with comfy Middle Eastern decor. *11am-10pm*

Simulatte $$

33 D3

This Turkish spot will stimu*latte* your palate with its tasty assortment of sweets, pastries, coffees and teas. Don't miss the mouthwatering walnut baklava. *8am-4pm Tue-Fri, 9am-5pm Sat & Sun*

Cheap Eats

Frieda $

 D6

This European-style restaurant offers fair-wage employment and excellent prices in a delightful space. The baked goods and breakfasts are delish. *8am-3pm Tue-Fri, from 9am Sat & Sun*

The Bourse $

35 C4

This mega-sized food court has just about any kind of food you could want, but it's the Mexican stalls that truly shine. *7am-8pm Mon-Sat, 9am-6pm Sun*

Desserts

Franklin Fountain $

36 F4

A classic parlor dishing up house-made ice cream, sundaes, milkshakes and old-fashioned soda fountain treats. *noon-midnight Sun-Thu, from 11am Fri & Sat*

Old City Coffee $

37 E3

Known for its artisanal coffee, this celebrated spot also has a nice selection of pastries, cookies and other baked goodies. *7am-4pm Mon-Thu, to 5:30pm Fri & Sat, 8am-5pm Sun*

Drinking

Coffee & Tea

Menagerie Coffee

38 D4

Clean, classy and brick-walled, this coffee shop is a favorite go-to for its range of espresso drinks, its relaxed European vibe, and the great snacks and sandwiches. *7am-5pm Mon-Thu, to 6pm Fri & Sat, 8am-5pm Sun*

La Colombe

39 B3

A Philly chain that's gone big, La Colombe offers great specialty coffees, a signature 'draft latte' and excellent indie vibes close to the Liberty Bell. *7am-6pm*

Gong Cha

40 E5

This spot specializes in bubble tea, offering a diverse menu of refreshing flavors and customizable options in a vibrant and modern setting. Don't be surprised if the line goes out the door. *10am-10pm*

Dive Bars

Khyber Pass Pub

41 E5

This divey pub not only has cheap beers and specials but also offers Cajun and New Orleans food that's hard to come by out East, such as red beans and rice. *11am-2am Mon-Fri, from 10am Sat & Sun*

Cocktails

Olde Bar

42 E6

A swanky spot featuring classic American seafood in a historic building and timeless cocktails, including all the Prohibition-era greats plus unique new takes, such as London Fog Sour. *4-10pm Tue-Sun*

National Mechanics

43 D4

In what once was the 1837 Mechanics National Bank, this bar now plies in liquid gold: cocktails that will slake the thirst of any high-end drinker. *noon-10pm Mon & Tue, to midnight Wed, noon-2am Thu & Fri, from 10am Sat, 10am-10pm Sun*

Panorama

44 F4

A wine-focused restaurant with an extensive selection of Italian vino and craft cocktails paired with classic Italian dishes and gorgeous panoramic views of the city. *5-9pm Tue-Thu, to 10pm Fri, 3-10pm Sat, to 9pm Sun*

48 Record Bar

45 E5

More casual than some of the Old City standbys but far swankier than a dive, 48 Record Bar has a nice music-first vibe and friendly bartenders. Cocktails are creative, surprising and reasonably priced. *5pm-2am Wed-Sun*

Shopping

Fashion

Rennes

46 E1

A once-Boston-based fashion label that moved to Philly and has become a standby. Sells women's clothing and outerwear, as well as some homewares, such as cups and teapots. *11am-6pm Tue-Sat*

Charlie's Jeans

47 D3

A denim-mostly spot with styles for men and women. If you need the latest bell bottoms or high-waisted

styles, chances are you'll find them here. *11am-4pm Mon-Sat*

Vagabond

48 E2

Stocks independent labels making pieces with natural fibers in earthy tones, as well as jewelry and accessories. *11am-6pm Mon-Sat, noon-5pm Sun*

Gifts & Souvenirs

3rd Street Gallery

49 F3

This artist-run co-op – actually on 2nd St – is one of the area's oldest galleries. The space also has tons of events and rotating exhibitions. *4-7:30pm Fri, 1-5pm Sat, noon-4pm Sun*

Humphry's

50 E2

If all this independence has you feeling patriotic, pick up a flag to wave in just about any size imaginable at this cute store. *9:30am-4:30pm Mon-Fri*

Philadelphia Independents

51 E3

Stocking a wide variety of affordable items by local artists, Philadelphia Independents is a great destination for original and quirky gifts and souvenirs. Its range includes cool T-shirts, jewelry, accessories, ceramics, prints and greeting cards. *11am-7pm*

Food

Shane Confectionery

52 F4

Willy Wonka would feel right at home in this historic candy store and confectionery selling ethically sourced, handmade chocolates, truffles and other sweet treats (pictured). *11am-7pm Sun-Thu, to 9pm Fri & Sat*

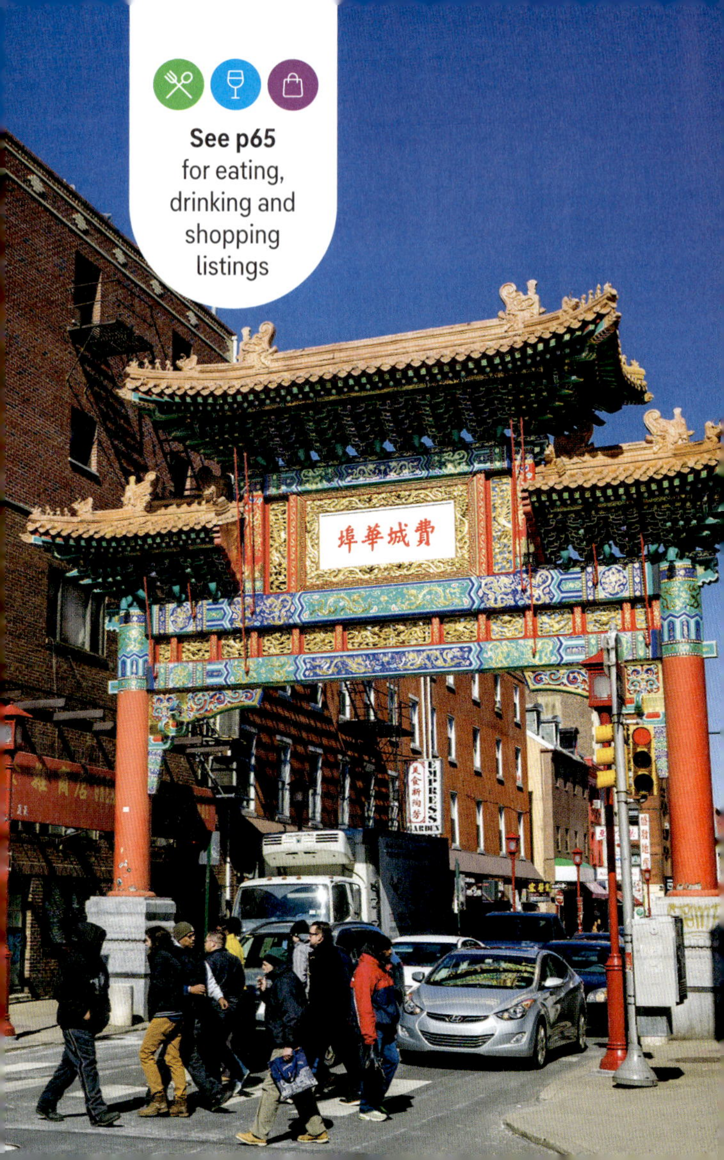

See p65
for eating, drinking and shopping listings

Explore Chinatown & the Gayborhood

Two fantastic foodie destinations are the star features of this central slice of Philly: the historic Reading Terminal Market and the fourth-largest Chinatown in the USA, both of which provide hungry visitors with tons of mouthwatering delights. LGBTIQ+ visitors in particular will feel comfortably welcome in the rainbow-flag-flying 'Gayborhood,' also known as Midtown Village. The Gayborhood's rainbows aren't just flying on flags from windows and rooftops: even the crosswalks are colorfully proud. The area is fun, festive and welcoming to all.

Getting Around

Bus

SEPTA buses crisscross these neighborhoods. Hop on the PHLASH bus along Market St.

Subway

Market-Frankford Line subway stations include 15th, 13th and 8th Sts. Broad Street Line trains stop at City Hall, connecting with the trolley to 13th St.

Train

Access SEPTA Regional Rail lines at the underground Jefferson Station. The PATCO line has stations at 9th/10th St and 12/13th St.

Bicycle

Electric-assisted bicycles rentable on Indego (rideindego.com) are ubiquitous. You can rent at one kiosk and return at another.

Chinese Friendship Gate (p55)

THE BEST

Slurp freshly made noodles in **CHINATOWN**, one of the oldest in the country. (p60)

Taste a cornucopia of foods in **READING TERMINAL MARKET**, the city's historic and cavernous market hall. (p58)

Gape in amazement at the architectural styles of the meeting halls in the **MASONIC TEMPLE**. (p61)

Dine, dance and see a drag show in Philly's inclusive **GAYBORHOOD**. (p60).

Walk Chinatown

Chinatown is delightful chaos, a mix of sights, smells, curbside vendors and bustling energy. A fun way to spend part of a day is a walk around the neighborhood, best experienced on a leisurely meander with plenty of stops along the way. In addition to the wonderful food, take in the evocative murals too.

START	END	LENGTH
Reading Terminal Market	Chinese Friendship Arch	0.6 miles, 1½ hours

1 Have Your Cake & Eat It Too

Exploring the food stalls at the massive indoor **Reading Terminal Market** could be its own walking tour, but it makes a good spot to begin a Chinatown walk. Enjoying the sights, smells and sounds, and then exit onto the corner of Arch and 11th Sts and follow 11th St north.

2 Oodles of Noodles

Turn east onto Race St to see stores with Chinese characters on the signs and more hustle and bustle than before. Keep walking, or if you're hungry, stop in at **Nan Zhou Hand Drawn Noodle House**, where a line often snakes out the door for delicious chewy noodles and other Chinese treats. This place is cash only, but it has an ATM.

3 History Writ Large

Turn north on 10th St and head north to Winter St. On one side is the Vine St Expwy, but look to the south to spot the ***History of Chinatown*** mural, which depicts the many conflicts Chinese Americans have faced in this city, such as exploitation by railroad companies and battles residents have fought to stay here.

4 A Sip of Bubble Tea

Many come to Chinatown to get their sweet tapioca pearl fix. **Chicha San Chen** is a top contender and has cute string-tied take-out cups that are popular. To try this treat, go east on Winter St to 9th St and turn south. Next, turn west on Race St.

5 Where Chinatown Started

Walking further west to 913 Race St, you'll find a signpost with a brief note about Chinatown's uniqueness in Pennsylvania. Look on the wall for the **Birthplace of Chinatown Marker**: this spot is where the original Chinese laundry stood.

6 Welcome to Chinatown

Turn south on 10th St. The spectacular **Chinese Friendship Gate** standing at the intersection of Arch and 10th Sts was a collaborative process between Sabrina Soong, a local Chinese-American artist, and one of Philly's sister cities, Tianjin, China, which provided materials. The gate marks a symbolic entrance to Chinatown and features several important Chinese symbols, such as dragon and animal motifs.

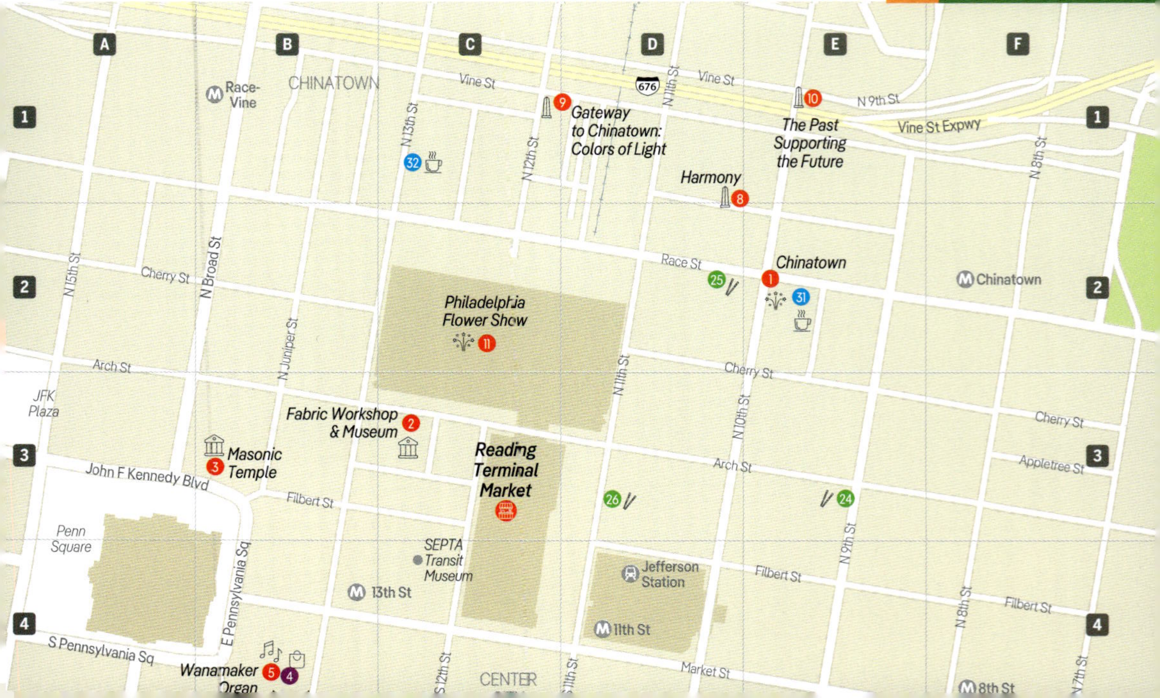

A
B
C
D
E
F
1
2
3
4
Race-Vine
CHINATOWN
Vine St
676
N 11th St
N 13th St
N 12th St
N 9th St
9 Gateway to Chinatown: Colors of Light
10 The Past Supporting the Future
Vine St Expwy
N 8th St
32
8 Harmony
Race St
25
1 Chinatown
31
Chinatown
N 15th St
Cherry St
N Broad St
N Juniper St
11 Philadelphia Flower Show
Arch St
N 11th St
Cherry St
N 10th St
JFK Plaza
2 Fabric Workshop & Museum
3 Masonic Temple
Reading Terminal Market
Arch St
Cherry St
Appletree St
John F Kennedy Blvd
Filbert St
26
24
Penn Square
E Pennsylvania Sq
SEPTA Transit Museum
Jefferson Station
Filbert St
N 9th St
13th St
N 8th St
Filbert St
11th St
S Pennsylvania Sq
Wanamaker Organ 5
4
S 12th St
CENTER
S 11th St
Market St
8th St
N 7th St

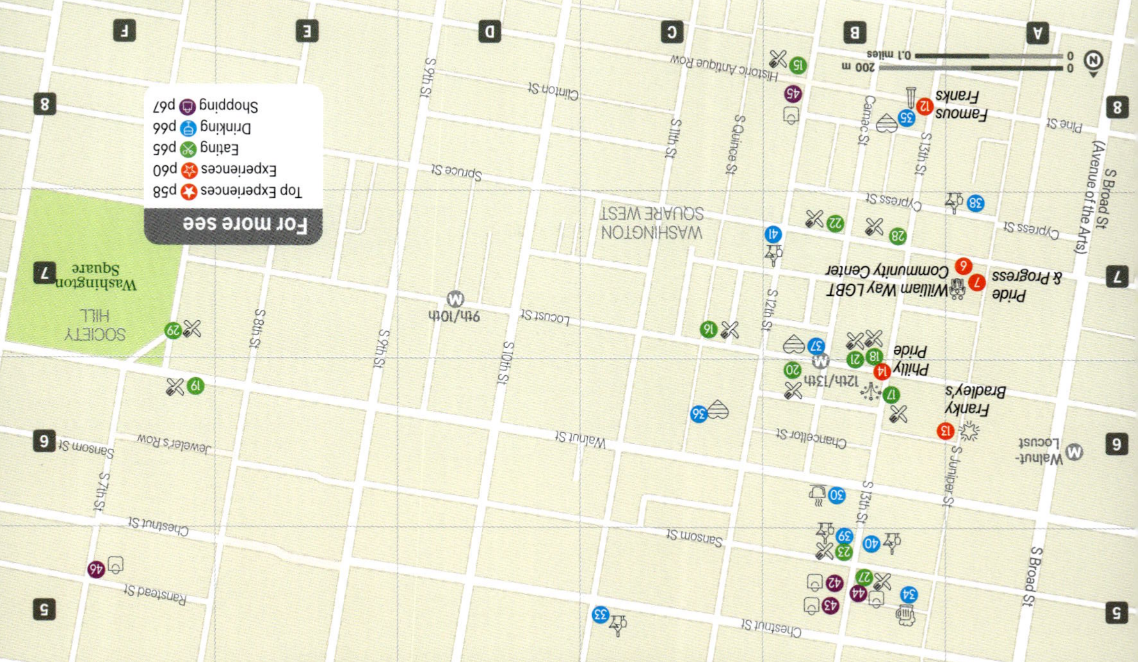
For more see
Top Experiences p58
Experiences p60
Eating p65
Drinking p66
Shopping p67
SOCIETY HILL
Washington Square
WASHINGTON SQUARE WEST
9th/10th
12th/13th
Walnut-Locust
Philly Pride
Franky Bradley's
William Way LGBT Community Center
Pride & Progress
Famous Franks
Chestnut St
Ranstead St
Sansom St
Jeweler's Row
Walnut St
Chancellor St
Locust St
Spruce St
Cypress St
Clinton St
Pine St
Historic Antique Row
Camac St
S 7th St
S 8th St
S 9th St
S 10th St
S 11th St
S Quince St
S 12th St
S 13th St
S Juniper St
S Broad St
S Broad St (Avenue of the Arts)
200 m
0.1 miles

★ TOP EXPERIENCE

Reading Terminal Market

Keeping the balance right between a food market and a dining destination, **Reading Terminal Market** dates from 1893 and is a city institution. The stalls provide strong flavors of Philly's cultural melting pot – from Pennsylvania Dutch to Asian cuisine – and attract visitors from billionaires to blue-collar workers.

MAP P56 **C3**

PLANNING TIP
Wander around the whole market before making a purchase. Otherwise, you might buy something only to take three steps and wish you had more stomach space.

Scan for opening hours and the market's vendor list.

Take It All In

Visiting Reading Terminal Market is an adventure for the senses, a feast for the eyes as much as for the tastebuds. The atmosphere is electric, with vendors hawking fresh produce, artisanal cheeses, international cuisines and handmade crafts from crowded, bustling market stalls. The scent of aromatic spices and freshly baked goods wafts through the air, and the energy is palpable as locals and tourists weave through the chaos looking for that perfect treat to munch on. Pick up Amish baked goods, handmade doughnuts, meats, cheeses, canned goods, soaps, clothing and more. Come back at different times of day because the vibe changes substantially from early morning to lunch to late afternoon.

Pick & Choose

Reading Terminal Market has nearly 100 stalls to check out, but you'll definitely want to try these top spots. Note that Amish and Mennonite stalls are closed on Sundays.

Bassetts The country's oldest ice-cream company, established in 1861.

Miller's Twist Known for its buttery pretzels.

DiNic's Dig into its succulent roast pork sandwich.

Dutch Eating Place Amish delicacies, breakfasts, lunches and baked goods.

F11PHOTO/SHUTTERSTOCK ©

Hershel's East Side Deli Jewish favorites including corned beef sandwiches and kosher apple cake.
Pearl's Oyster Bar Freshly shucked oysters, spicy pepper pot and snapping turtle soup.
Beiler's (pictured) Hot-from-the-fryer doughnuts and apple fritters, plus bread and barrels of pickles.
Sweet Nina's Incredibly tasty banana pudding.
PA General Store Stocks both food and nonfood items produced in the state.

Go on a Tour

Snack and listen to Philly food lore on a 45-minute market visit with **City Food Tours** (phillysfood tour.com). Tours begin at 10:30am and 2pm, kick off with a treat from a vendor and end with an additional something to savor.

TAKE A BREAK
Press pause on your feasting and head to the SEPTA Transit Museum. It's more of a room than a full museum, but it has interesting exhibits about Philadelphia's public transport system.

EXPERIENCES

Spend a Beautiful Day in the Gayborhood

AREA

Whether you're gay or straight, Philly's beloved **Gayborhood** always has something for you to see, do or experience, day or night. This area stretches from Chestnut to Pine Sts and from Broad to 11th Sts and is filled with shops, restaurants, bars and clubs proudly flying rainbow colors and welcoming all. Look up, down and around and you'll see rainbows everywhere: hanging from windows and atop flagpoles – even the crosswalks are done in the colors of Pride.

Start the day with a spectacular meal at one of the breakfast and brunch spots, such as **Sofi Corner** (p65). If you're here during lunch or dinner hours, the area has some of Philly's best restaurants, including **Kiddo** (p65). After dark, the Gayborhood becomes a playground of entertaining drag shows, dive bars, dance clubs and swanky spots to sip a good cocktail. In this inclusive, welcoming place, anyone can let loose and enjoy themselves.

Ring in the Chinese New Year

FESTIVAL

MAP: 1 P56 E2

The fourth-largest **Chinatown** in the USA celebrates Asia's biggest holiday (chinatown-pcdc.org) in January or February with exciting lion dances, a parade, and much eating and drinking. The streets fill with jubilant crowds, and wafts of special Chinese New Year foods like noodles, golden spring rolls, fish and buns delight the nostrils. Lion dances start at 10th and Race Sts and wind their way through the district, with firecrackers and festivities.

Chinese New Year is a time of togetherness. Families flood the restaurants, gather to pay respects to ancestors, exchange red envelopes for good luck, and dig into traditional dishes that symbolize prosperity and abundance. Many shops offer free gifts, and troupes of dancers parade from store to store, hoping for tips. Just about everything will be red and gold, colors that in China symbolize what the Lunar New Year is all about: hopes for wealth and prosperity to come.

Learn About Textiles at the Fabric Workshop & Museum

MUSEUM

MAP: 2 P56 C3

Step into the **Fabric Workshop & Museum** (fabricworkshopandmuseum.org, suggested donation $5) and be immersed in a rich tapestry of exhibits showcasing diverse textile traditions from around the globe. From ancient fabrics and traditional garments to contemporary textile innovations, each display tells a story of cultural heritage, artistic expression and technological advancement.

A lot of this museum is hands-on, and interactive exhibits let you touch, feel and even create your own fabric masterpieces. Visitors also have the opportunity to witness live demonstrations of weaving, dyeing and embroidery techniques.

Admire the Architecture at the Masonic Temple HISTORIC BUILDING

MAP: 3 P56 **B3**

Although the fortress-like exterior of the 1873 **Masonic Temple** (pamasonictemple.org, adult/child $15/5) is impressive, it's the spectacular interiors – which took a further 15 years to complete – that blow visitors away. Fans of secret societies and architecture will be in rapture when they see the meeting rooms, each of which sports an astonishingly detailed theme: Moorish, Egyptian, Renaissance and more.

Freemasonry's roots in Philadelphia stretch back to colonial times. In the library, where tours of the building start and finish, you can view George Washington's Masonic apron. German immigrant George Herzog did most of the mural paintings and primary designs, and the Masonic Temple was one of the first buildings in the city lit by electricity.

Dine in Style on 13th Street AREA

Part of the Gayborhood, **13th St** is known for its wealth of dining spots. Philadelphia is blessed when it comes to food, but if you want to head to a spot where you can't trip without falling into a great restaurant, 13th St from Walnut to Lombard is 'Restaurant Row.' It's not just the number of restaurants but also the diversity, and it's all here, from Indian to Italian, Greek to Georgian, and French to fine American. Top spots to dine include **Vetri Cucina** (p66) (vetricucina.com), **Bud & Marilyn's** (p65) (budandmarilyns.com) and **Green Eggs Cafe** (p65) (greeneggscafe.com).

Listen to the Wanamaker Organ at Macy's LIVE MUSIC

MAP: 4 P56 **B4**

Like many department stores, **Macy's** (macys.com) has had a rough go as of late, with many

PHILADELPHIA GAY MEN'S CHORUS

The Philadelphia Gay Men's Chorus (pgmc.org) has delivered engaging and thought-provoking performances to more than 100,000 listeners since 1982, when it began as a group of three gay men who went door-to-door caroling at Christmas. The group is instrumental in raising LGBTIQ+ awareness and acceptance in Philadelphia and has several outreach programs to help the LGBTIQ+ community. The men have sung at many places, such as baseball stadiums, community centers and even City Hall, and their performances often include sing-alongs and audience participation.

stores slated for closure. Let's hope that the one on Market and 13th escapes the axe because it's a Philly institution, both for its incredible pipe organ and its role in one of the city's biggest festivals.

Back in 1909 when Macy's was Wanamaker's, owner John Wanamaker installed the enormous Wanamaker Organ (MAP: 5 P56 **B4**) (wanamakerorgan.com), hosting free concerts to delight shoppers and encourage them to linger. The tradition lives on, with classical and pop tunes filling the department store's central atrium at noon and 5:30pm. While you're hanging around Macy's Grand Court, check out Eagle, a 1904 bronze statue that's a popular Philly meeting point.

The department store also hosts the fun **Christmas Light Show** from Thanksgiving (late November) to New Year's Eve, when the Grand Court atrium is heavily decorated with trees, lights, candles and ornaments. The animated figures are a hit with kids.

WILLIAM WAY LGBT COMMUNITY CENTER

MAP: 6 P59 **A7**

A cornerstone of the Gayborhood is the dynamic **William Way LGBT Community Center**, which hosts a range of events and activities from art shows and music festivals to skills classes and support, many of them for free.

Pride and Progress

MAP: 7 P59 **A7**

Filling the west wall of the center is a tribute to the Gayborhood in which it stands, a vibrant 2003 mural by Ann Northrup called Pride and Progress. The main subject is a Pride festival, but on the right, a poster shows a gay civil rights march from 1966, a mark of how far the community has come.

Marvel at Chinatown's Murals

PUBLIC ART

MAP: 8 P56 **D1**

Philly's **Chinatown** is covered in murals. At 1034 Spring St, the *Harmony* mural shows a group of multicultural children in a circle holding hands. About a block away at 247 N 12th St, the *Gateway to Chinatown: Colors of Light* (MAP: 9 P56 **C1**) mural peeks out from behind a more recently built structure that blocks it. You can still get a view if you peer sideways at it on N Sartain St. It's a shame that such a dynamic piece of art was covered up, but murals, just like the residents of Chinatown, have always had to fight for survival.

A tall building rises on the northern side of Vine St Expwy. *The Past Supporting the Future* (MAP: 10 P56 **E1**), a stunning 2023 mural with a red background and a crane, graces its western facade.

See Floral Works of Art at the Philadelphia Flower Show EVENT

MAP: 11 P56 C2

Taking place in March, the colorful and wildly popular **Philadelphia Flower Show** (phsonline.org/the flower-show) started in 1829. It has grown into a huge Philly event, and the displays are extravagantly over the top. Every year, the features are different and in previous years have included a massive display with sculptures highlighting the beauty of water, flower neighborhoods' based on Philly's own, many workshops, discussions and a trade show area for vendors.

Hundreds of thousands of people come to see the themed displays, but this event wasn't always about creating flowerful displays. It was here that the poinsettia, a favorite Christmas flower, was first introduced to a welcoming audience.

Watch a Drag Show in the Gayborhood LIVE PERFORMANCE

Catching a drag show in the **Gayborhood** is a highlight of visiting Philly. They're big, brash, flamboyant and saucy, and audiences are often left in stitches. Beer and cocktails are on the menu, but what's really served are fun, fancy outfits, big hair and big booties.

Each drag show is different. Some performers focus on dance numbers and show tunes, while others do standup or offer moving tales of their experiences. Many drag show performers are local celebrities, but others come from around the country, performing on tour. Don't think that if you've seen one show, you've seen them all.

Franky Bradley's (frankybradleys.com, MAP: 13 P56 **A6**) is a Gayborhood standby, known for its 'dancing, DJs, and deviation,' as well as cheap beers and excellent food. **Bob and Barbara's Lounge** (p82) (bobandbarbaras.com) is a standby, with nightly drag shows, live music, burlesque and its famous 'Special,' a shot-and-beer combo at a ridiculously low price. (It's technically not in the official 'Gayborhood' but on nearby Broad St.)

FAMOUS FRANKS

MAP: 12 P59 **B8**

On the wall outside of the iconic watering hole Dirty Franks, the Famous Franks mural has faces of 19 people with 'Frank' in their names, from Aretha Franklin to Pope Francis and Frank Sinatra. Other notable Franks, all of which are connected in some way to either the painter or the city, include Frank Oz, Frank Zappa, a frankfurter, Frankenstein's monster and Frank Sherlock, a Dirty Franks employee and locally known poet. Two of the Franks, Pope Francis and Frank Sherlock, were added when the mural was restored in 2015.

Show Your True Colors at Philly Pride

FESTIVAL

MAP: 14 P56 B6

The entire month of June features **Philly Pride** (pictured) events in one of the city's biggest and most extravagant celebrations. The festivities kick off with a huge parade, starting at 6th and Walnut Sts and ending in the Gayborhood. Because it takes place at the start of the summer season, clothing can be vastly more skimpy than on the similarly festive Mummer's Parade, which happens in January.

Rainbows are everywhere, and revelers of all stripes pack the streets. It's a party for all, with hilarity, fun and a bit of the risqué. While the focus is on pride and the LGBTIQ+ community, everyone is welcome to take part.

Philly Pride features food trucks, shows, events, buskers and performances. There are tributes to the Latinx LGBTIQ+ community to specifically promote this slice of the community to widen visibility.

In the 1980s, Philadelphia fought on the front lines of the AIDS/HIV epidemic, and its citizens were among the first to be diagnosed and shunned as fear of the disease spread. In some ways, this history makes Philly Pride one of the city's most important celebrations.

Best Places for...

$ Budget $$ Midrange $$$ Top End

Eating

Breakfast & Brunch

Kiddo $$

 B8

The surprising flavor combinations turn brunch (often full of the familiar) into an exciting adventure that leaves you full (portions aren't small) and eager to return. *4-10pm Wed-Mon, 10am-2pm & 4-10pm Sat & Sun*

Sofi Corner $$

16 C7

A delightful LGBTIQ-friendly spot, with a pretty patio in the back or tables (often crowded) inside. The *shakshuka* (a Middle Eastern dish of poached eggs and tomatoes) is particularly good. *8am-5pm*

Green Eggs Cafe $$

17 B6

Tasty, local and unique, Green Eggs Cafe has all the traditional breakfast favorites, plus creative takes such as red velvet pancakes and birthday cake French toast. Cash only. *9am-3pm Mon-Fri, to 4pm Sat & Sun*

Cheap Eats

Bud & Marilyn's $$

18 B7

Great breakfasts, succulent and crispy fried chicken, mouthwatering hanger steaks that will stick to your ribs: it's all good here. *5-10pm Mon-Thu, to 11pm Fri, 10am-3pm & 5-11pm Sat, to 10pm Sun*

Knead Bagels $

19 F6

Freshly baked New York–style bagels with creative spreads and toppings like *togarashi* (Japanese pepper and spice blend) or flax. It has vegetarian options as well. *7:30am-1:30pm Tue-Fri, 8am-1pm Sat & Sun*

Vegan & Vegetarian

Vedge $$

 B6

If you've been shy about going vegan and want to see it done spectacularly, visit Vedge. You'll leave delighted, sated and inspired. The menu belies its plant-based origins. *5-9pm Tue-Sat*

Italian

Little Nonna's $$

21 B7

Cozy and cute Italian spot on Locust St with alfresco dining, garden tables or cozy red leather inside. The food is hearty and authentic, and the desserts make you feel like you're in Italy. *5-10pm*

Mercato $$

22 B7

Creative, inspired Italian food served in hearty quantities, with Old World caliber and interesting modern twists. This spot is homey, airy and satisfying. *4:30-9:30pm Sun-Thu, to 10:30pm Fri & Sat*

Mexican

El Vez $$

23 B5

Fresh and authentic Mexican food served in a restaurant that's so colorful you may need to put sunglasses on. *11:30am-10pm*

Asian

Banh Mi Cali $

24 E3

American-sized banh mi at a cash-only spot, as well as bubble tea. Look for the orange awning. *11am-7pm*

Nan Zhou Hand Drawn Noodle House $

25 D2

Expect to wait for a table at this popular noodle shop, where everything on the menu is good, but the bowls of cut noodles in savory broth are the pièce de résistance. *11am-10pm*

Tom's Dim Sum $

26 D3

You can eat dim sum cheaply, but it's surprisingly easy to keep on ordering as these morsels (usually served in threes or fours) go down so easily. The soup dumplings are particularly popular. *11am-10pm Sun-Thu, to 10:30pm Fri & Sat*

Fine Dining

Barbuzzo $$

27 B5

This packed, delicious restaurant serves dishes from Italy and across the Mediterranean. Portions run smaller than at some spots, but that means you have room to order more – and you'll want to *5-10pm Mon-Thu, to 11pm Fri, 11am-3pm & 5-11pm Sat, 11am-3pm & 4-10pm Sun*

Vetri Cucina $$$

28 B7

Offering one of the priciest meals in Philly, this spectacular spot has a gourmet prix fixe that's divine. Pairing the dishes with the wine selection is highly recommended. *5-9pm*

Talula's Garden $$$

29 F7

Next to Washington Square, this spot serving seasonal American cuisine uses farm-to-table ingredients, and tables are set in an elegant garden. *5-10pm Mon-Fri, from 4pm Sat, 10am-2pm Sun*

Drinking

Coffee & Tea

Cafe Square One

30 B6

A well-located coffee stop near Center City, with a nice selection of pastries, sandwiches and caffeine choices. *7am-5pm Mon-Fri, 8am-3pm Sat-Sun*

Chicha San Chen

31 E2

This Chinatown bubble tea spot has taken Philly by storm, with impressive teas and cute little string handles for carrying the cups. *noon-9pm Sun-Thu, to 9:30pm Fri & Sat*

Premium Steap

32 C1

A secret spot for tea lovers, this spot (a little hard to find behind the warehouse-like exterior) has fine teas from all over the world. The owner is a wealth of tea knowledge. *10am-5pm Mon-Fri*

Pubs & Bars

MilkBoy Philadelphia

33 C5

An icon of Philly's bar scene, with open mic nights, live music and food in addition to the drinks. Come because you're thirsty – stay for the vibe. *11am-midnight*

McGillin's Olde Ale House

34 B5

Come for the friendly welcome and the Irish pub vibe rather than the food, which is skippable. *11am-2am*

LGBTIQ+ Nightlife

Dirty Franks

35 B8

Everything you could want in a friendly neighborhood gay bar, including cheap drinks, drag shows and dartboards. *4pm-2am Mon & Tue, from 1pm Wed-Sun*

Bike Stop

36 C6

A Philly icon, this leather-and-chains gay biker bar is not for 'beginners.' It's not uncommon to see someone walking around in a harness and not much else. *4pm-2am Mon-Sat, from 2pm Sun*

U Bar

37 B7

Popular gay bar with food and great pours. The vibe is quiet and conversational rather than frenetic. *11am-2am*

Wine & Cocktails

Writer's Block Rehab

38 A7

Word-play heavy decor and good craft cocktails that even Hemingway would approve of. *4-8pm Mon, 5-11pm Wed & Thu, 4-11:30pm Fri & Sat, to 9pm Sun*

Charlie Was a Sinner

39 B5

This spot has good cocktails that suit the needs of any tippler. Try the banana-flavored Beast of Burden. *4-11pm Sun-Thu, to 2am Fri & Sat*

Double Knot

40 B5

The ambiance, service, dishes and cocktails are top notch. *4-10pm Sun-Tue, to 11pm Wed & Thu, to midnight Fri & Sat*

Tria Cafe Wash West

41 B7

A great spot to grab a glass of wine and unwind after a long day. Its 'happier hour' is a big draw. *4-9:30pm Mon-Thu, to 10pm Fri, 2-10pm Sat, to 8:30pm Sun*

Shopping

LGBTIQ+

Duross & Langel

42 B5

Gay-owned and operated, with wonderful soaps and lotions made in small batches on-site. *11am-5pm Wed-Fri, to 3pm Sat, Sun & Tue*

Open House

43 B5

Excellent for gifts and souvenirs, such as mini versions of the *LOVE* sculpture, as well as lots of Pride-themed items. *11am-7pm Mon & Tue, to 8pm Wed-Sat, noon-6pm Sun*

Verde

44 B5

Lesbian-owned boutique of gifts and curiosities, such as incense and jewelry. *11am-7pm Mon-Sat, noon-6pm Sun*

Philly AIDS Thrift @ Giovanni's Room

45 B8

Proclaims itself as the 'oldest and very best LGBTQ & feminist bookstore in the country,' and it might be right. *11am-8pm Mon-Sat, to 7pm Sun*

Food

Lore's Chocolates

46 F5

A charming neighborhood chocolatier with Philly-themed items, such as Liberty Bell–shaped chocolates, as well as more standard chocolates, all handmade. *10am-5pm Mon-Fri, from 11am Sat*

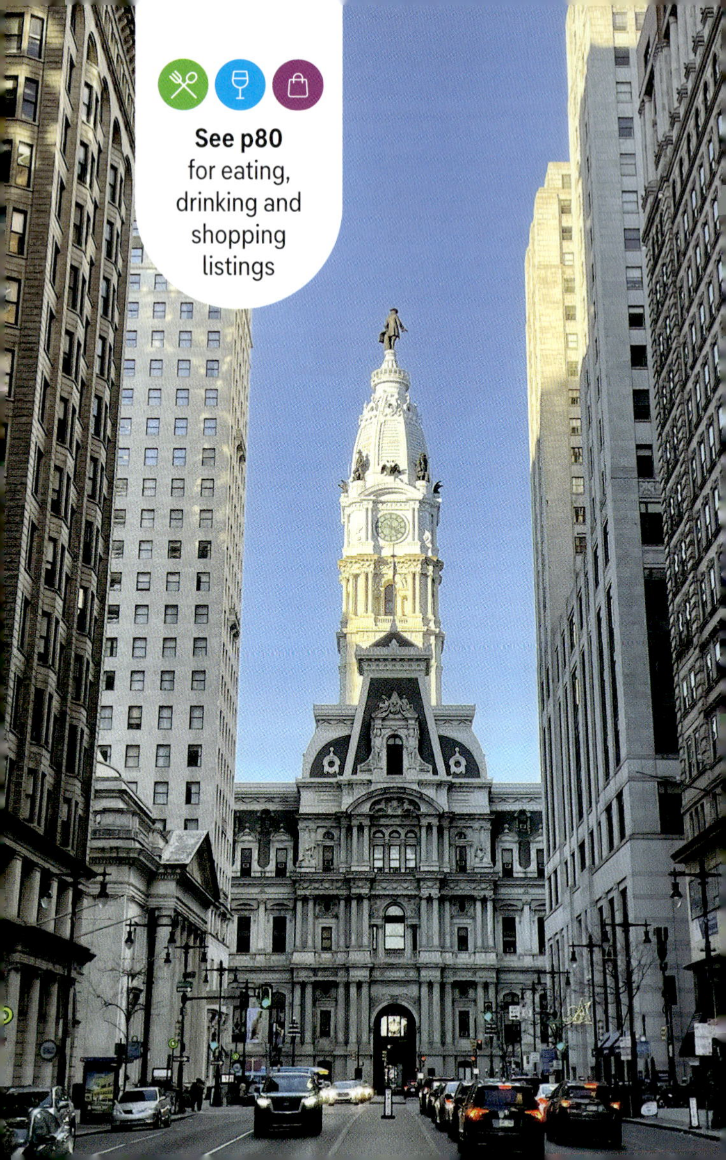

See p80
for eating,
drinking and
shopping
listings

Explore Rittenhouse Square & Center City West

'ew city centers are as magnificent as Philadelphia's, where the tunning, ornate City Hall is topped by a William Penn statue ınd festive international flags greet people on Benjamin Franklin 'kwy. The surrounding blocks are the engine of Philadelphia's conomy: offices, big hotels, concert halls and restaurants.

Just a few blocks southwest, genteel Rittenhouse Sq is a quiet ounterpoint, an elegant residential district dotted with cafes and mall restaurants. Between the two ıre the prime retail strips of Chestıut and Walnut Sts. This area is both he prime attraction for sightseers ınd a bit rough-and-tumble.

THE BEST

Marvel at the view from the clock tower at **CITY HALL** (p74) and gaze up at the giant statue of William Penn.

Squirm at the collection of anatomical and pathological specimens and medical artifacts at the **MÜTTER MUSEUM** (p75).

Experience the craziness that is the **MUMMERS PARADE** (p74) on January 1 each year.

Be wowed and dazzled by tech wonders at the **COMCAST CENTER** (p79).

Getting Around

Bicycle

lent a bike for an hour at a time using the ıdego app (rideindego.com). Ride for up to n hour and then return it at one of the kiosks nd rent another one if you need to.

Bus

EPTA buses crisscross these neighboroods. Access the PHLASH bus around ;ity Hall.

Subway

Market-Frankford Line subway stations ıclude 15th and 13th. Broad Street Line 'ains stop at City Hall, Walnut-Locust and ombard-South.

;ity Hall (p74)

WALKING TOUR

Walk Center City

Ever since the city commissioned a 37ft bronze statue of William Penn to go atop the City Hall building in 1892, public art has been central to Philadelphia's civic project. This walk around Center City takes you past key commissions. Build in extra time if you want to tack on a tour of City Hall.

START	END	LENGTH
Lenfest Plaza	A Quest for Parity	0.5 miles, 45 minutes

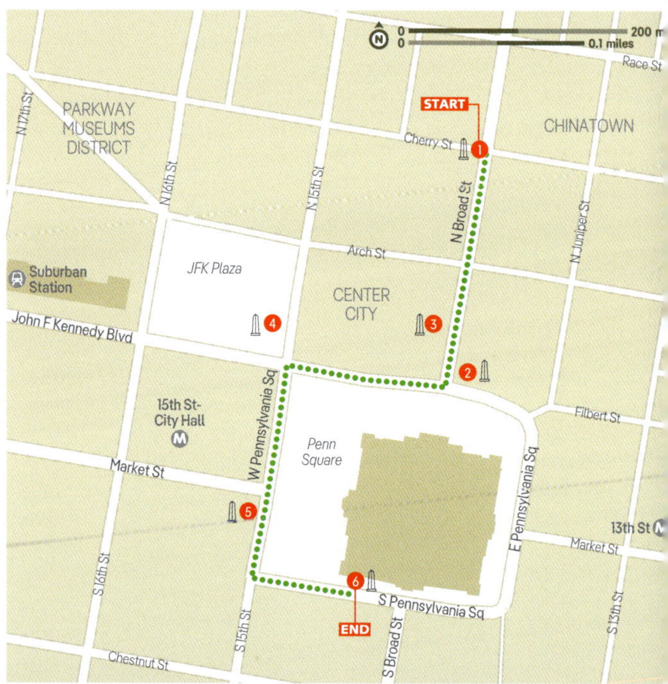

1 A Lick of Paint

n Lenfest Plaza is Claes Oldenburg's *'aint Torch*, a 51ft fiberglass ›aintbrush with an accompanying ;iant blob of paint. It's a work hat either delights or disgusts: 'or some, it's a quirky symbol of vhat makes city sculpture great. 'or others, it's cartoonish and ›verhyped.

2 The Bond of Friendship

ust outside the Masonic Temple, ***'he Bond*** is a bronze statue lepicting two close friends, George Vashington and Benjamin Frank-in. It's often mistakenly viewed as he two men shaking hands, but culptor James West intended to how a ceremonial masonic apron ›eing passed from one leader to he other.

3 Questioning Democracy

'he broad **Municipal Services 3uilding Plaza** opposite City Iall hosts several public artworks, ncluding the massive bronze *Jovernment of the People* by acques Lipchitz, which represents he struggle for democracy. It's challenging piece to observe nd seems unbalanced, unwieldy nd contorted. People are twisted together in an attempt to keep a heavy weight aloft.

4 Fall for LOVE

Have your camera ready for one of Philly's most popular selfie locations: in front of Robert Indiana's iconic ***LOVE* sculpture** in JFK Plaza.

5 Larger than Life

Find another eye-catching piece by Claes Oldenburg: the giant ***Clothespin***, a 45ft rendering of the standard household object. The steel and stainless structure almost appears to be a couple dancing in close embrace. It's often lit evocatively at night.

6 Sacrifice for Equality

A Quest for Parity: The Octavius V Catto Memorial is the first monument in the city dedicated to an individual Black person. A successful activist who led the battle to desegregate Philly's public trolleys, Catto was just 32 when he was killed on election day in 1871 while rallying Black men to vote. The impressive statue shows Catto standing, palms up, as if in the middle of giving one of the rousing speeches he was famous for.

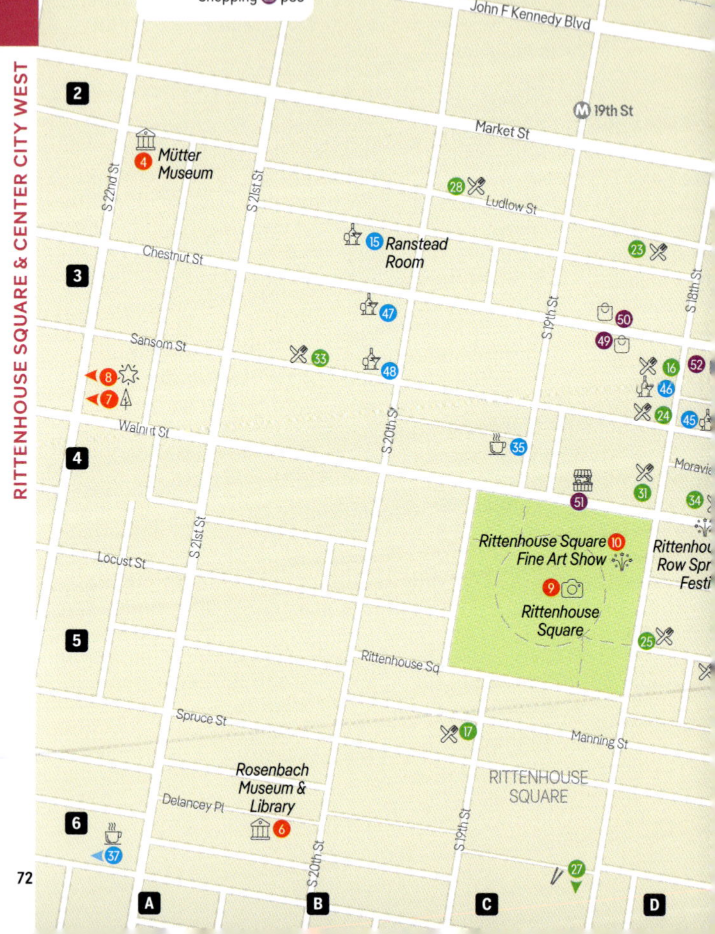

A
B
C
D
1
2
3
4
5
6
For more see
Experiences p74
Eating p80
Drinking p82
Shopping p83
Arch St
N 20th St
N 19th St
John F Kennedy Blvd
19th St
Market St
Mütter Museum
S 22nd St
S 21st St
Ludlow St
Ranstead Room
Chestnut St
S 19th St
S 18th St
Sansom St
Walnut St
S 20th St
Moravia
Rittenhouse Square Fine Art Show
Rittenhouse Square
Locust St
Rittenhouse Sq
Spruce St
Manning St
RITTENHOUSE SQUARE
Rosenbach Museum & Library
Delancey Pl

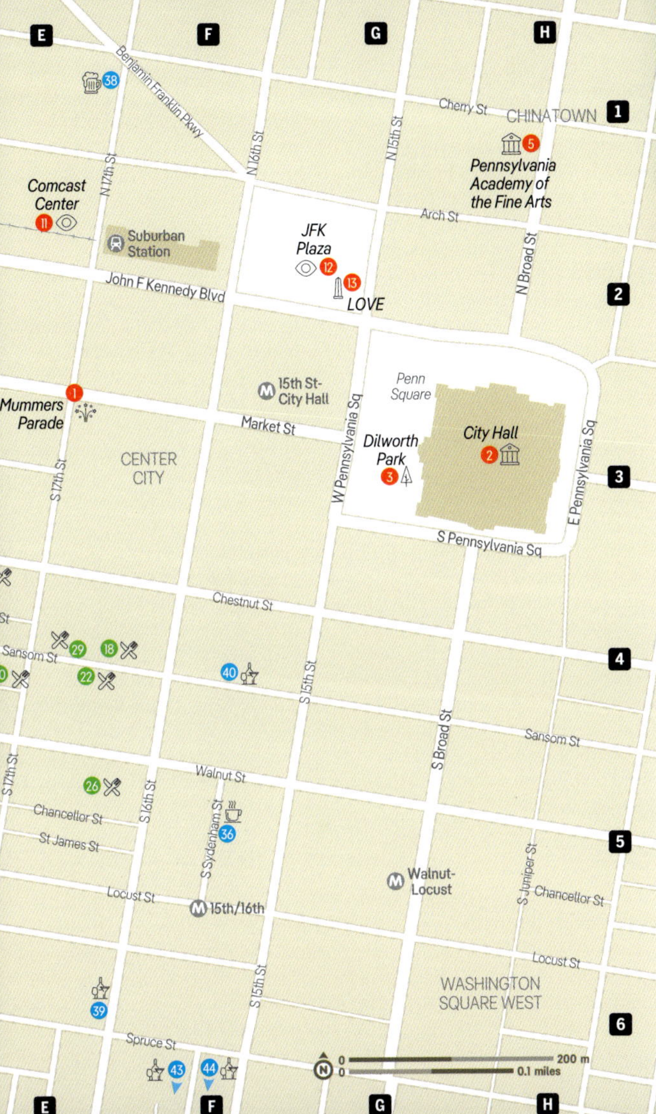
E
F
G
H
Benjamin Franklin Pkwy
38
Cherry St
CHINATOWN
1
5
Pennsylvania Academy of the Fine Arts
N 16th St
N 15th St
N 17th St
Comcast Center
11
Suburban Station
JFK Plaza
12
13
LOVE
Arch St
N Broad St
John F Kennedy Blvd
2
15th St-City Hall
Penn Square
Mummers Parade
Market St
W Pennsylvania Sq
Dilworth Park
3
City Hall
2
E Pennsylvania Sq
CENTER CITY
S 17th St
3
S Pennsylvania Sq
Chestnut St
Sansom St
29
18
20
22
40
S 15th St
4
S Broad St
Sansom St
S 17th St
Walnut St
26
S 16th St
Chancellor St
St James St
S Sydenham St
36
5
Walnut-Locust
S Juniper St
Chancellor St
Locust St
15th/16th
Locust St
WASHINGTON SQUARE WEST
S 15th St
39
6
Spruce St
43
44
0 200 m
0 0.1 miles

EXPERIENCES

Go Wild at the Mummers Parade

FESTIVAL

MAP: 1 P72 E3

The spectacular, colorful and dazzling **Mummers Parade** is a cross between Mardi Gras and a marching band competition. Thousands of people dress up, perform slapstick skits and comic plays, and ride the parade floats while thousands more watch the celebration. This event is unique to Philly and a must-see if you're in the area on January 1.

The tradition has its roots in Swedish and Finnish culture. Groups of holiday revelers would visit their neighbors after Christmas, and even in the time of George Washington, the tradition was well established. Mummers Parade performers fall into divisions – Fancies, Comic, Wench Brigades, Fancy Brigades and String Bands – each with its own role. Colorful costumes range from jester-like fools to drag and evening gowns.

With the multiple road closures and traffic jams, chances are you won't be able to get away from it even if you wanted to. The parade starts at 17th and Market Sts and moves toward City Hall before continuing on Broad St and finishing at Washington Ave.

Meet William Penn at City Hall

HISTORIC BUILDING

MAP: 2 P72 H3

For many Philadelphia visitors, taking a tour of **City Hall** (phlvisitorcenter.com/CityHall) is a trip highlight. The building is impressive to look at from afar, but it's even more amazing when you get to hear some of the tales that have taken place within these storied walls.

Completed in 1901 following 30 years of construction, City Hall takes up a whole block, and at 548ft is the world's tallest structure without a steel frame. The view from the observation area immediately beneath the 27-ton bronze statue of William Penn that crowns the tower takes in most of the city. Visit on the **City Hall Tower Tour**

MURAL ARTS TOURS

A lot of Philly's larger-than-life art is not in a gallery but staged around the city – murals on walls are everywhere. The Mural Arts Program aims to further its namesake artform for the city and its people. To gain more insight, join one of its tours, most of which start from the lobby of the Pennsylvania Academy of the Fine Arts. Knowledgeable guides lead these walking or trolley-based tours between April and the end of November, covering murals in a specific location or on a particular theme. The Mural Mile, a free self-guided tour and map, is available online at muralarts.org/self-guided.

Mummers Parade

(adult/child $16/10) or the full two-hour **Interior & Exterior Tour** (adult/child $36/30), which includes the tower. Space is limited, so reserve tickets well in advance.

Ice-Skate at Dilworth Park PARK

MAP: 3 P72 G3

On the west side of City Hall, Dilworth Park (centercityphila.org/parks/dilworth-park) is a compact public area that has a cafe, seating and free internet access. In summer, water spouts dance in the fountain, and in winter, the **Rothman Ice Rink** fills with skaters, from just-learning toddlers and hand-in-hand couples to the hockey and figure-skater types who make everyone else look bad.

Skates are available to borrow. Although the rink gets busy, it's still a lot of fun for young and old. If it's snowing, you'll feel like you're in a Hollywood rom-com.

Say 'Eww!' at the Mütter Museum MUSEUM

MAP: 4 P72 A2

Maintained by the College of Physicians, the unique, only-in-**Philadelphia Mütter Museum** (muttermuseum.org, adult/child $20/15) is an attraction dedicated to rare, odd and disturbing medical conditions. Want to see a life-size

RACE MATTERS

Philadelphia is one of the most segregated cities in the USA, as well as one of the poorest. The geographical and economic divisions between ethnic groups in Philly are stark and controversial. The Black Lives Matter movement upped the ante on such discussions. One of its targets was the statue of controversial former Mayor Frank Rizzo. Activist Asa Khalif voiced the feelings of the wider Black community when he said the statue represented decades of oppression and violence. In 2020, the statue was removed from its prominent location facing City Hall.

wax example of the stages of syphilis? You've come to the right place.

Though this museum is not for the squeamish, it's not just going for shock value. Adults and budding junior scientists and physicians will find it educational, interesting and, sure, pretty gross.

Exhibits include a saponified body, a conjoined female fetus, incredibly realistic wax models of medical conditions and skulls by the dozen, as well as descriptions of the now thoroughly debunked theory of phrenology, the pseudo-science that claimed (wrongly) that the size and shape of a person's skull dictated his or her abilities. Another exhibit explores the parallels between the 1918 Spanish Flu epidemic and COVID-19, with insightful history and analysis.

The museum is housed in a compact space, but its fascinating subject matter means you'll likely spend two to three hours here.

See Paintings at the Pennsylvania Academy of the Fine Arts

MUSEUM

MAP: 5 P72 H1

The prestigious **Pennsylvania Academy of the Fine Arts** (pafa.org, adult/child $18/10), an art school founded in 1805, occupies two buildings, including a masterwork of Victorian Gothic architecture designed by Frank Furness and George Hewitt.

Start your tour of the museum's collection in that building (closed temporarily until fall 2025), where the interior design nearly – but not quite – overshadows the works on display. The sculptures are so life-like that they seem to watch as you tour the galleries, which include famous works by Winslow Homer, Andy Warhol and Mary Cassatt.

Continuing education classes allow the public to dive in and experience art by making instead of viewing. Sculpture and painting classes and other workshops take place frequently, so check the calendar (pafa.org/museum/events).

Check Out the Book Selection at the Rosenbach Museum & Library

MUSEUM

MAP: 6 P72 **B6**

The list of famous authors in the collection at the **Rosenbach Museum & Library** (rosenbach.org, adult/child $12.50/7.50) could fill a book itself: Edgar Allan Poe, James Joyce, Maurice Sendak, George Washington, Lewis Carroll and Bram Stoker, to name a few. If you fancy a peek at an original copy of Ulysses, this is the place.

Admission includes a guided tour through the museum and library. Tours, which allow access to rare and important items not usually on display, are offered at 3pm most Fridays and Sundays. Register online two weeks in advance.

Take a Kayak Tour of Schuylkill Banks

KAYAKING

MAP: 7 P72 **A4**

Schuylkill Banks (pronounced SKOOL-kill) is a wonderful outdoor recreation area that covers about 8 miles of the **Schuylkill River** (MAP: 8 P72 A4), mostly on the east bank below the **Fairmount Dam** through the heart of Philadelphia. It offers fantastic outdoor fun in a surprising location: right in the center of the city.

One of the best ways to enjoy this unique area is on a guided kayak tour. Set off with **Hidden River Outfitters** (hiddenriveroutfitters.com) and paddle the river with an experienced guide, learning about the history and ecology of this riparian area. If you'd rather get on the water without the work, riverboat tours are also available. Check the Schuylkill Banks website (schuylkillbanks.org/events/riverboat-tours) for dates.

Have Fun Below the Flags on Benjamin Franklin Pkwy

STREET

The broad, sweeping diagonal **Benjamin Franklin Pkwy** extends from **JFK Plaza** (p79) in a northwest line to the **Philadelphia Museum of Art** (p90), and both sides of the road are festooned with flags from around the world. Learn about flags and challenge your flag-identification skills while strolling or cycling along this pretty street.

HOMELESSNESS IN PHILADELPHIA

Homelessness is an issue in Philadelphia. Philly has one of the highest poverty and unemployment rates in the country. Housing doesn't come cheap, and the lack of affordable places to live has pushed more people onto the streets. About 50% of Philadelphians pay more than a third of their income on rent, an indicator of the disparity between well-paying work and housing market prices. Being unhoused also has a racial component. In a 2023 survey, 72% of people experiencing homelessness were Black, even though Black people make up only 40% of the city's residents.

Rittenhouse Square

Meander Around Rittenhouse Square

SQUARE

MAP: 9 P72 D5

One of five original squares planned by city founder William Penn in the late 17th century, **Rittenhouse Square**, the most prestigious, was originally known as Southwest Square. It was later renamed after David Rittenhouse, an 18th-century astronomer, mathematician and clockmaker.

It features a fine collection of bronze statues, a kids wading pool and benches beneath shady trees.

Buy Local Pieces at the Rittenhouse Square Fine Art Show

EVENT

MAP: 10 P72 D5

Taking place since 1928, the outdoor **Rittenhouse Square Fine Art Show** (rittenhousesquareart.com) showcases paintings, etchings, drawings and sculptures for sale, and is one of the oldest art shows in the country. Over the years, the show has been raided by police (for nudity), targeted by Communist sympathizers (for propaganda) and endured hard times during World War II.

Today, it features almost 150 different artists from the Philly area. Come to support local artists, get great deals on artwork and perhaps even get an original by the next big name in the art world.

Step Inside a Cinematic Sphere at the Comcast Center NOTABLE BUILDING

MAP: 11 P72 **E2**

The giant glass-clad **Comcast Center** (comcastcentercampus.com) is one of the tallest 'green' buildings in the USA. Its 140ft-tall atrium lobby is the location of Humanity in Motion, a beguiling work consisting of 10 horizontal poles crisscrossing the space on which life-sized figures balance like tightrope walkers.

Attractions at the Comcast Center change, but one of the coolest at the moment is a giant geodesic dome known as the **Universal Sphere**. Inside is a small 3D movie theater, an immersive experience that packs a punch. Though only 15-minutes, it's well worth checking out, especially for families.

Find *LOVE* at JFK Plaza PLAZA

MAP: 12 P72 **G2**

Officially called **JFK Plaza**, **Love Park** (MAP: 13 P72 G2) takes its nickname from Robert Indiana's iconic *LOVE* sculpture, which stacks the letters of the word in candy-apple red. In winter, the statue looks great when it's wearing a white coat of snow. In addition to the art, the plaza also has a fountain for cooling off in summer and orange chairs to sit in.

Fun fact: the plaza was designed by architect and city planner Edmund Bacon, father of the actor Kevin Bacon.

Hop into the Rittenhouse Row Spring Festival FESTIVAL

MAP: 14 P72 **D4**

Every May, the streets around Rittenhouse spring alive with booths, tables and merriment during the **Rittenhouse Row Spring Festival**. Billed as the city's 'most upscale event,' it's a great way to welcome the season, with live music, food and drink, and a fashion show.

Do Your Best to Find Rittenhouse's Speakeasies COCKTAIL BAR

MAP: 15 P72 **B3**

Some of Philadelphia's best bars can be found in this neighborhood, but they can be easy to overlook. **Ranstead Room** (ransteadroom.com) is one of several Philly speakeasies that hearken back to Prohibition. You won't find any signs outside, just a dim red lantern above a doorway next to some dumpsters.

Place your name on the reservations list for that night only (Ranstead Room doesn't take advance reservations). Once you've been given a time, you can leave to have dinner or drinks elsewhere until you get a text.

LISTINGS

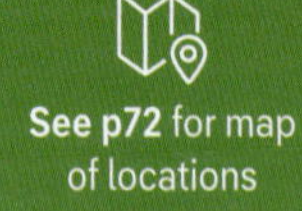
See p72 for map of locations

Best Places for...

$ Budget $$ Midrange $$$ Top End

Eating

Breakfast, Brunch & Lunch

Cleavers $$

 16 D3

Devour incredible cheesesteaks and a whole lot more at this popular sandwich spot that offers artisanal ingredients and even a vegan cheesesteak option made with portobello mushrooms. *11am-9pm Sun-Wed, to 10pm Thu-Sun*

Metropolitan Cafe & Bakery $$

 17 C6

From 'power' muffins and almond croissants to delicious bagel breakfast sandwiches, this corner spot has all you need to start a great day. Specialty pizzas and sandwiches make it popular for lunch as well. *7:30am-3pm Mon & Wed-Sat, from 8am Sun*

Square 1682 $$

18 E4

Inside the Hotel Palomar, this restaurant has hearty breakfasts, tasty mains and nice drinks throughout the day. *7am-10pm*

Green Eggs Cafe $$

19 D3

Mammoth portions make Green Eggs hard to beat if you're looking for a meal that will stick to your ribs well into the afternoon. Delicious French toast, eggs and waffles make it easy to find something satisfying. *9am-3pm Mon-Fri, to 4pm Sat & Sun*

North American

Luke's Lobster $$

20 E4

Part of a casual East Coast chain serving authentic tastes of Maine using sustainably sourced seafood. Wash down your buttered-bun lobster roll with a wild blueberry soda. *11am-8pm*

Mulberry $$

 21 D1

American fare and tasty cocktail options at this spot with high ceilings, a long and airy bar, and the feeling that you've stepped into a Hopper painting. *11:30am-2am Tue-Sun*

Federal Donuts & Chicken $$

 22 E4

This delightful icon has a variety of craft doughnut flavors that change daily, as well as great fried chicken. *7am-8pm*

El Techo $$

23 D3

This fun, festive Mexican joint has good food, but the drinks and – even better – the rooftop city views are what make it really shine. *4-10pm Wed & Thu, to 12:30am Fri, noon-12:30am Sat, 10:30am-4pm Sun*

Around Europe

Dandelion $$

24 D4

This British-themed pub has great cocktails, a homey bar where it's easy to meet new friends, and excellent food, including Welsh rarebit and bangers and mash. *11:30am-11pm Mon-Thu, to midnight Fri, 10am-midnight Sat, to 10pm Sun*

Parc Brasserie $$

25 D5

Beloved haute French bistro cuisine with white doily curtains, starched napkins and impeccable service. Creamy, decadent sauces and elevated flavor pairings transport you to France. *8am-10pm Mon-Thu, to 11pm Fri, 10am-11pm Sat, to 10pm Sun*

Pizza Vetri $$

26 E5

A delightful spot for inventive pizzas and calzones. Folks rave about the margherita. Thanks to its Neopolitan-style process that includes fermenting the dough, no two pies are exactly alike. *11:30am-9pm Sun-Thu, to 10pm Fri & Sat*

Middle Eastern & Asian

Octopus Falafel Truck $

27 C3

Hard to believe a simple food truck could offer so much great flavor. Get super Middle Eastern falafel, chicken skewers and other tasty specialties. *noon-2:30pm Mon-Fri*

Southgate $$

28 D6

Bibimbap, a rice dish in a heated stone bowl, is highly recommended, as is the KFC (Korean fried chicken). Plenty of fresh side dishes supplement the main. *4-10pm Tue-Thu, to 11pm Fri, 2-11pm Sat, to 10pm Sun*

Dizengoff $

29 E4

Incredible Israeli food by chef Mike Solomonov. Creamy, buttery takes on hummus, exquisite combinations of spices and flavors you can't find elsewhere, and attentive service. It's all top notch. *11am-2pm & 5-11pm Sun-Wed, to midnight Thu-Sat*

Vegan & Vegetarian

PS & Co $$

 D5

Not only is this pleasant cafe vegan and gluten-free, it's also kosher to boot. Breakfast dishes are served all day. The barbecue tempeh burgers and Burmese chickpeas shine. *8am-4pm Mon-Fri, 10am-5pm Sat & Sun*

Fine Dining

The Love $$$

 D4

Fall in love with the menu at The Love, which ranges from fried chicken to a vegan platter. The latter is not just simmered veggies; it's a lovely exploration even nonvegans enjoy. Desserts are sublime. *11:30am-2pm Mon-Fri, from 10am Sat & Sun*

Gran Caffè L'Aquila $$$

32 E4

Be transported to old-world Italy. Surprise and delight your tastebuds with savory gelato (think cold sauces) and perfectly done Italian specials. *7am-10pm Mon-Thu, to 11pm Fri, 8am-11pm Sat, to 10pm Sun*

Bolo $$$

33 B3

This spot by a James Beard–nominated chef is a delightful romp through Latin American cuisines, from Caribbean ceviches to chicken *ropa vieja* (shredded meat in a thick tomato stew), elevated to art with flavors that will surprise. *5-10pm Sun-Fri, to midnight Sat*

a.kitchen+bar $$$

34 D4

Stunning New American plates with impeccable flavor combinations make this place shine. No wonder it's a James Beard winner. *8am-3pm & 4:30-9pm Sun-Thu, to 10pm Fri & Sat*

Drinking

Coffee & Tea

La Colombe

35 C4

An indie powerhouse, this Philly original chain invented the draft latte (its signature coffee) and has delicious teas and espressos as well. Rittenhouse is the original, where it all began. *7am-7pm*

Elixr Coffee Roasters

 F5

This hopping coffee spot has a warehouse theme, complete with meat-locker doors for the bathrooms. Good wi-fi and quality hand-dripped coffees make it a fun stop. *7am-7pm*

Rival Bros Coffee Bar

37 A6

Hand-pours over house-roasted beans make Rival popular, as well as its selection of locally made pastries, bread and chocolates. *6am-6pm Mon-Fri, from 7am Sat & Sun*

Pubs & Bars

Con Murphy's

 E1

This classic Irish pub on the ground floor of the Windsor Suites has a good beer selection and surprisingly good cocktails for a spot competing with far ritzier places. *11am-midnight*

Monk's Cafe

39 E6

Hop fans crowd this mellow wood-paneled place for Belgian and American craft beers on tap – it has one of the best selections in the city. For those needing assistance, a 'Beer Bible' is available. *11:30am-11:45pm Tue-Sun*

Harp & Crown

 F4

Upstairs, this buzzing restaurant and bar has a double-height ceiling and long horseshoe bar, but downstairs there's a two-lane bowling alley and cozy gentleman's club–like space with leather armchairs. *4pm-midnight*

City Tap

 E1

Kick back and enjoy the excellent selection of beers, both bottled and on tap. It also serves typical tavern fare, but the drinks are the reason to come. *11:30am-10pm*

LGBTIQ+

Stir Lounge

42 E5

This friendly, 'everyone's welcome' gay bar is tiny and divey but special for going against the ritzy Rittenhouse vibe and just being a fun hangout spot that instantly makes you feel at home. *3pm-1am Tue, 4pm-2am Wed-Sat, to midnight Sun*

Bob & Barbara's Lounge

 F6

A cheap spot with a popular, long-running drag show. The Philly 'special' (PBR and a shot of Jim Beam for $3) is a permanent fixture. *4pm-2am*

Wine

Jet Wine Bar

 F6

This futuristically decorated wine bar takes its flights seriously, aiming to transport you to different regions of the world. Bottle specials and truly unique pairings make it a treat. *5-10pm Wed-Thu, to midnight Fri, 4pm-midnight Sat*

Tria Cafe

45 D4

The original outpost of this popular wine bar is a dark, elegant and welcoming place with excellent cocktails and snacks. It's LGBTIQ+ friendly, and the food pairings are a cut above. *4-9:30pm Mon-Thu, noon-10pm Fri & Sat, 11am-8:30pm Sun*

Cocktails & Speakeasies

Ranstead Room

15 B3

A delightful speakeasy with elevated craft cocktails and a dimly lit bar that transports you back to Prohibition. *7pm-midnight Mon-Wed, to 2am Thu-Sat*

Franklin Mortgage & Investment Company

46 D4

Expect a line leading to the unmarked door at this elevated speakeasy named for a notorious Prohibition-era alcohol purveyor. Be aware that some drinks cost more than $100. *5-11pm Sun-Thu, to 2am Fri & Sat*

1 Tippling Place

47 B3

Lots of armchairs and sofas make this a relaxing, comfy spot. Cocktails are top-notch without being overly pricey. *5-10pm Tue-Thu, to midnight Fri & Sat*

Village Whiskey

48 B3

A fine bar perfect for stopping in for an afternoon tipple, evening meal or nightcap. It's known for its selection of about 200 whiskeys from around the world, and its cocktails are tasty too. *4-10pm Tue-Fri, 10am-3pm & 4-10pm Sat & Sun*

Shopping

Fashion

Boyd's

49 D3

Boyd's has been in business since 1938, initially specializing in men's clothing but later branching into womenswear. It's a grand space to browse and buy designer labels. *11am-6pm Mon-Sat*

Joan Shepp

50 D3

Not for the faint of pocketbook, this chic womenswear boutique offers a roll call of designers from Comme des Garçons to Rick Owens. *11am-6pm Tue-Sat*

Food & Souvenirs

Rittenhouse Farmers Market

51 D4

Along the north side of Rittenhouse Sq, stalls sell fresh fruit and veggies, bread and baked goods, pickles, preserves, flowers, and hand-painted chocolates at this Saturday market. *10am-2pm Sat*

Di Bruno Bros

52 D3

If you're after gourmet food items, such as olive oils, coffee, crackers, jams and cheeses, this impressive grocery/deli is almost sure to have it. *7am-8pm Mon-Sat, to 7pm Sun*

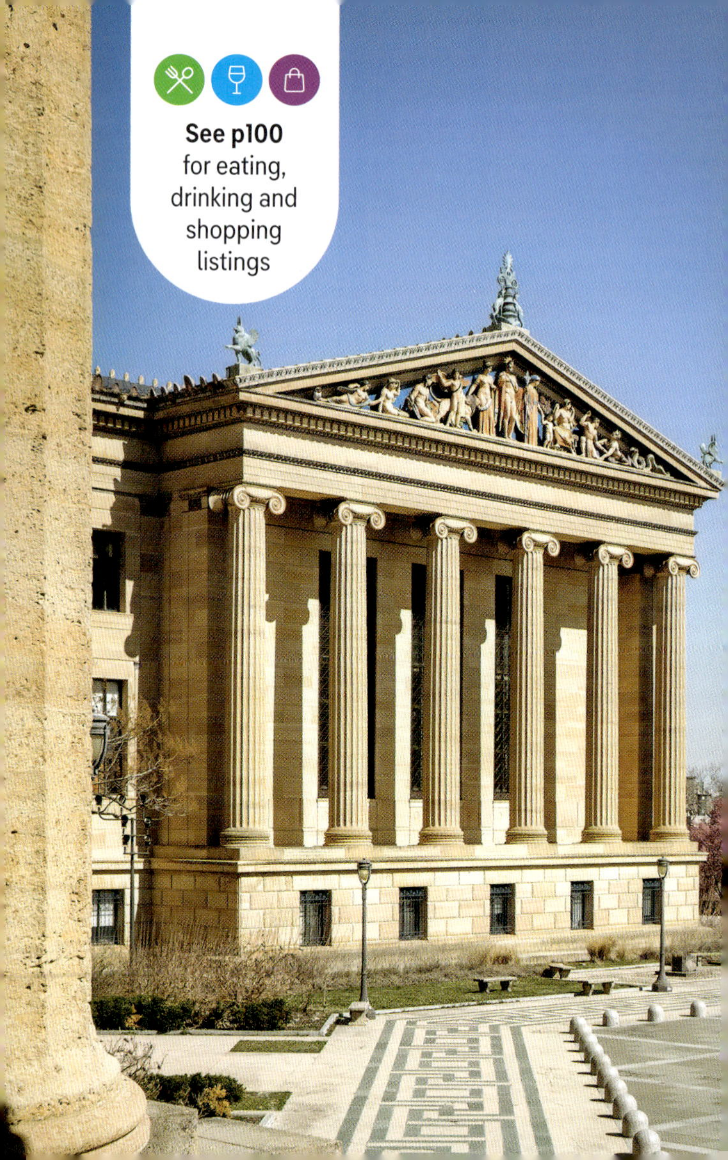
See p100
for eating,
drinking and
shopping
listings

Explore Logan Square & Fairmount

Benjamin Franklin Pkwy is the location of many of the city's most treasured cultural institutions, including the magnificent Philadelphia Museum of Art and 2000-acre Fairmount Park. This street is where the Mummers Parade festivities kick off. Logan Square and Fairmount are rich areas for art and science, and the Academy of Natural Sciences museum is a prime attraction. The neighborhood is full of interesting architecture, evocative streets and alleyways, and it's peppered with excellent spots to eat. Its central location makes it a great hub for exploring almost anywhere in Philadelphia.

Getting Around

Bus

Useful SEPTA buses include 7, 27, 33, 38, 43, 48 and 49. The PHLASH bus also covers Benjamin Franklin Pkwy to and from Logan Sq, Eastern State Penitentiary and (on a separate service) west Fairmount Park.

Bicycle

Rent a bike through the useful bike-share app Indego (rideindego.com).

Trolley

Route 15 connects with the Philadelphia Zoo.

Train

SEPTA Regional Rail lines serve Suburban station. Use East Falls and Wynnefield Ave stations for Fairmount Park.

Philadelphia Museum of Art (p90)

E4 PLUS/SHUTTERSTOCK ©

THE BEST

Explore the **PHILADELPHIA MUSEUM OF ART**, home to one of the best collections in the country (p90).

Ponder incarceration policies at **EASTERN STATE PENITENTIARY**, an eerie former prison (p92).

Swoon at the Cézanne, Degas, Matisse, Renoir and Van Gogh canvases on display at the **BARNES FOUNDATION** (p94).

Cycle, jog or simply stroll through **FAIRMOUNT PARK** (p95).

Cycle Fairmount Park

This tour of Philly's central green lung follows part of the Schuylkill River Trail cycling paths on the east and west banks. If you don't want to explore on two wheels, you can walk, drive or even kayak the route, and see several of the sights. The closest Indego bike rental is at 27th and Philadelphia.

START	END	LENGTH
Boathouse Row	Laurel Hill Cemetery	4.5 miles; 1½ hours

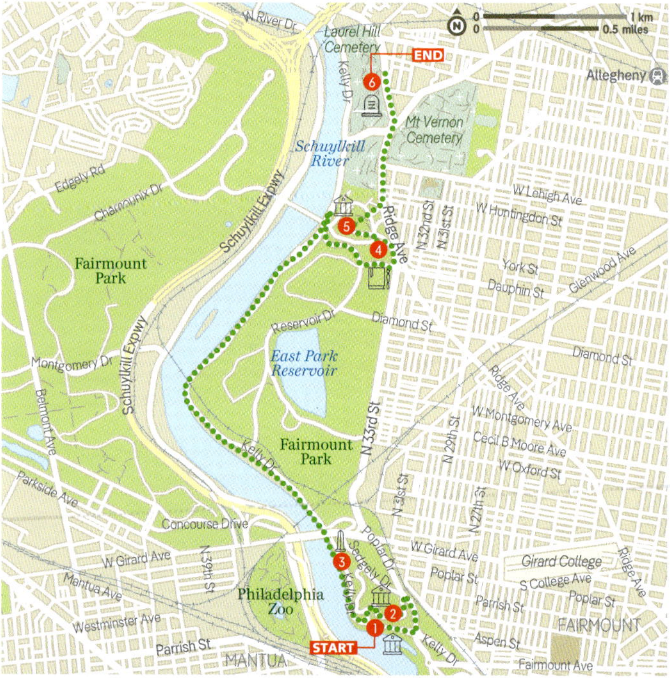

1 Smooth Sailing

Boathouse Row, a picturesque strip of mock Tudor and Victorian buildings, isn't just sitting pretty – it's an active part of river life, housing the craft of many of the waterway's rowing clubs. In the evenings, the structure outlines are lit up, reflecting festively in the water. Check boathouserow.org for the clubs' racing schedule.

2 When Life Gives You Lemons

Lemon Hill, a mansion built in 1799, is one of several preserved within Fairmount Park. It's named after the lemon trees that once grew in the greenhouses that were on the estate in the early 19th century, though you won't find any now. Inside, you'll find that the Federal-style building is notable for its stack of oval rooms and views of the city skyline.

3 Seeing Sculptures

The **Ellen Phillips Samuel Memorial**, a riverside garden section of the park, comprises three terraces decorated with 17 sculptures that were commissioned between 1933 and 1961. Though many of the sculptures are stunning, the pieces don't reflect the country's racial and cultural diversity because of the prevailing views at the time. Impressive pieces include Jacques Lipchitz's *Spirit of Enterprise* and Wheeler Williams' *The Settling of the Seaboard*.

4 A Colonial Getaway

Begun in 1756, the Georgian **Woodford Mansion** was built in several stages and completed in the 1770s as a summer retreat for William Coleman, a Philadelphia merchant and judge. Join a guided tour to see its fine collection of colonial furniture and decorative art.

5 Appreciate Antiquities

The largest historic house in Fairmount Park, **Strawberry Mansion** combines Federal and Greek Revival architecture. It's home to some fine antiques and art, including porcelain, furniture and Victorian dolls.

6 Six Feet Under

Founded in 1836, **Laurel Hill Cemetery** is the final resting place of numerous prominent Philadelphians, including 18th-century astronomer David Rittenhouse (the namesake of Rittenhouse Sq) and Victorian-era architect Frank Furness. Sign up for a guided tour (Friday to Sunday) or download the free Laurel Hill Cemetery app for self-guided tours of the 78 acres.

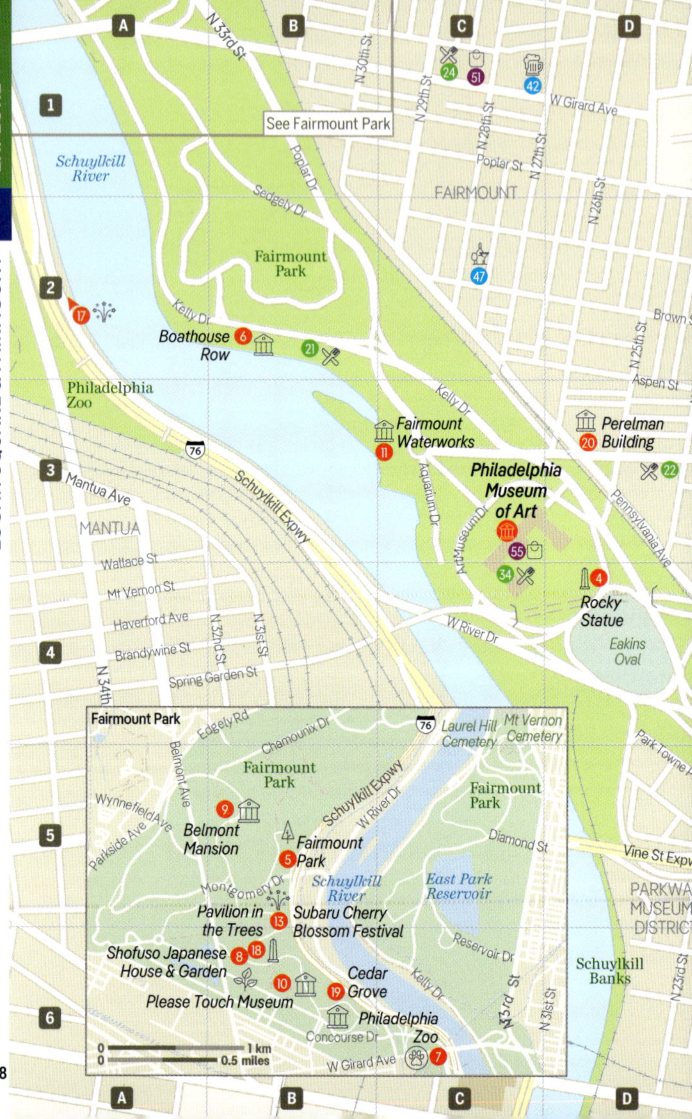
See Fairmount Park
Schuylkill River
Fairmount Park
FAIRMOUNT
Boathouse Row
Philadelphia Zoo
Fairmount Waterworks
Perelman Building
Philadelphia Museum of Art
Rocky Statue
Eakins Oval
MANTUA
PARKWAY MUSEUMS DISTRICT
Schuylkill Banks
Fairmount Park
Laurel Hill Cemetery
Mt Vernon Cemetery
Belmont Mansion
Fairmount Park
Schuylkill River
East Park Reservoir
Pavilion in the Trees
Subaru Cherry Blossom Festival
Shofuso Japanese House & Garden
Cedar Grove
Please Touch Museum
Philadelphia Zoo
0 1 km
0 0.5 miles

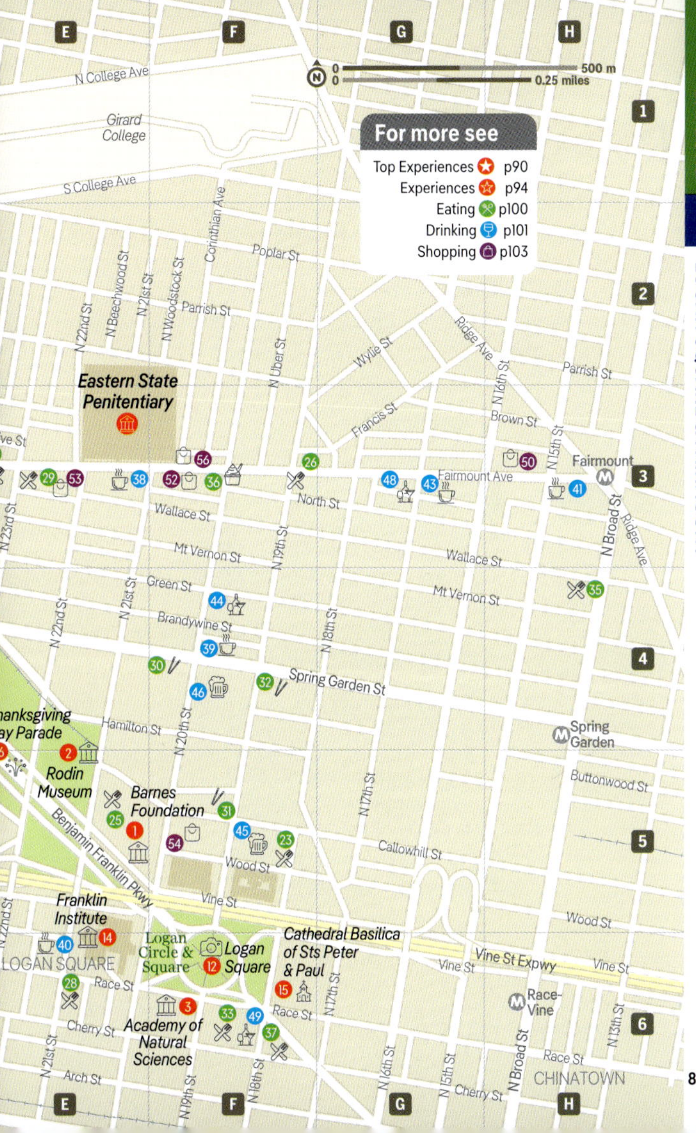

N College Ave
Girard College
S College Ave
500 m
0.25 miles
For more see
Top Experiences p90
Experiences p94
Eating p100
Drinking p101
Shopping p103
Eastern State Penitentiary
Fairmount
Spring Garden
Rodin Museum
Barnes Foundation
Franklin Institute
Logan Circle & Square
Logan Square
Cathedral Basilica of Sts Peter & Paul
Academy of Natural Sciences
LOGAN SQUARE
CHINATOWN
Race-Vine
Benjamin Franklin Pkwy
Vine St Expwy
Spring Garden St
Fairmount Ave
Ridge Ave

★ TOP EXPERIENCE

Philadelphia Museum of Art

The **Philadelphia Museum of Art**, the city's premier cultural institution, occupies a Grecian temple–like building housing a superb collection of Asian art, Renaissance masterpieces, postimpressionist works and modern pieces. Especially notable are galleries filled with complete architectural ensembles, including a medieval cloister and a Japanese teahouse.

MAP P88 **C3**

PLANNING TIP
On the first Sunday of each month and Fridays after 5pm, the museum has a pay-what-you-want policy, so you can save by visiting at these times. Otherwise, admission is $30.

Scan to book tickets and see opening hours.

American Art

The museum has a spectacular 12,000-piece collection of American art from colonial times to the modern day. A few highlights to look for are *Portrait of Dr Samuel D Gross* (also known as The Gross Clinic) by Thomas Eakins, *The Life Line* by Winslow Homer, *Yarrow Mamout* by Charles Willson Peale and a teapot made by Paul Revere. Georgia O'Keefe fans will delight in seeing *Two Calla Lilies on Pink*, one of her many stunning works.

Contemporary Art

Appreciating contemporary art takes a bit more effort from the viewer, but the museum offers a depth and breadth unparalleled in its collection. The collection includes pieces by Andy Warhol, Edna Andrade, Bruce Nauman, Zoe Leonard and many others, with thousands of works in its collection that are not currently on display.

Asian Art

Among hundreds of stunning works of ceramic art, silk scrolls and clothing is Sunkaraku, a real Japanese teahouse constructed in 1917 by Ōgi Rodō, his only work done outside Japan. The rooms display Japanese zen ideals, the concepts of simplicity and

ANDREA IZZOTTI/SHUTTERSTOCK ©

peacefulness, and harmony with the ceremony being performed.

Take a Tour

Many of the museum's tours, from in-depth looks at Rodin's hands to surveys of museum highlights and women in art, are free with your admission. Some tours are timed, so plan ahead if you want to join.

Save Your Ticket

Tickets to the Philadelphia Museum of Art are valid for two days and also include entry to the **Perelman Building** (p99), which hosts good rotating exhibits devoted to photography, fashion, art and design, and the **Rodin Museum** (p94), housing a superb collection of works by the French sculptor Auguste Rodin.

QUICK BREAK

The museum has two on-site cafes and a restaurant. If you want to get outside, try **Little Pete's**, a 10-minute walk away. The cheesesteaks can't be beat.

★ TOP EXPERIENCE

Eastern State Penitentiary

Tours of the eerie and fascinating **Eastern State Penitentiary**, a former prison, are a Philadelphia favorite year-round but especially at Halloween. A visit is more than a look into the past because exhibits explore issues that the country still grapples with today, such as racial prejudices and overcrowding.

MAP P88 **E3**

PLANNING TIP
The comprehensive free audio tour is worth a listen. Pick up headphones at the Visitor Services Desk. To have plenty of time for photos, set aside at least two hours.

Scan to book tickets and see opening hours.

Like Spokes on a Wheel

This prison was built like a giant asterisk, with all the structures originating from a point in the center. This design allowed one guard to stand in the center and easily monitor the entire prison by rotating around – he could check on all the hallways and respond quickly if problems arose. Other creative ways that guards kept tabs on the inmates involved strategically placed mirrors so that it was easy to see around corners and check that nobody was hiding behind a wall.

Changing Views, Changing Fortunes

When it opened, the Eastern State Penitentiary was seen as a paragon of modern incarceration, lauded by politicians, police and correctional institution directors. It offered something no other prison did at the time: solitary confinement, then seen as a miraculous solution to the unsafe practices of housing prisoners in dorms. But it was as costly as it was impressive, and as views on solitary confinement shifted, so too did the prison's fortunes.

Despite housing Al Capone and several other high-profile criminals, Eastern State Penitentiary began closing in 1960 and finally shuttered in 1971. Today, the beautiful decay of its eerie hallways, disused cells strewn with trash, peeling paint and

4KCLIPS/SHUTTERSTOCK ©

rusted bars are a favorite for photographers. The prison has great spots for photos almost everywhere you look, and those with a fondness for urban exploration will find it easy to spend hours here.

ESP's Legacy

It's impossible to visit Eastern State Penitentiary, wander through its galleries and learn about prisoners' stories without being confronted by ESP's legacy and the state of prisons today. Many parts of the judicial process in the United States have discriminated against people of color, from profiling, traffic stops and arrests, to jail sentences, incarceration and the death penalty. In a courtyard where prisoners once gathered for their allotted brief period of fresh air now stands an exhibit bringing many of these questions to the viewer.

QUICK BREAK
Head across the street to **OCF Coffee House** for espresso drinks and some unusual latte flavors, such as rose cardamom, as well as vegan options.

EXPERIENCES

Marvel at the Barnes Foundation

MUSEUM

MAP: 1 P88 **E5**

In the first half of the 20th century, collector and educator Albert C Barnes amassed a remarkable trove of artwork by Cézanne, Degas, Matisse, Renoir, Van Gogh and other European stars. Alongside, he set beautiful pieces of folk art from Africa and the Americas, an artistic desegregation that was shocking at the time. Today's **Barnes Foundation** (barnesfoundation.org, adult/child $30/free) is a contemporary shell, inside which is a faithful reproduction of the galleries of Barnes' original mansion (still in the Philadelphia suburbs).

The art is hung according to Barnes' vision, a careful juxtaposition of colors, themes and materials. Even more remarkable: you've likely never seen any of these works before because Barnes' will limits reproduction and lending. Though most of the rooms have static displays, one portion of the gallery is a rotating exhibit.

Admission is free on the first Sunday of the month. Tickets (only available online at members .barnesfoundation.org/vip) are limited to four per person, and there's a focus on family activities.

ROCKY BALBOA

MAP: 4 P88 **D4**

Philadelphia local Sylvester Stallone not only starred in the 1976 Oscar winner *Rocky*, but he also wrote the screenplay. A major Philly selfie spot is the 1980 statue *Rocky* by A Thomas Schomberg. The statue was created for a scene in Rocky III and had various locations around town before ending up back in its spiritual home next to the Museum of Art steps in 2006. The movie went on to be the actor-author's life-defining franchise.

Appreciate a Master at the Rodin Museum

MUSEUM

MAP: 2 P88 **E5**

Walking through the incredible **Rodin Museum** (rodinmuseum.org, suggested donation $15) is as close as you can get to meeting Auguste Rodin himself. You'll see not only versions of some of his most famous works but also many of the unknown, lesser works that give insights into his craft.

Administered by the **Philadelphia Museum of Art** (p90), this space is the only institution outside of Paris dedicated to the French sculptor, and its superb collection is based on works amassed by Jules E Mastbaum in the 1920s. The 140 sculptures from

PHILADELPHIA MARATHON

One way to see pretty much all of the city's landmarks in a day is to take part in the Philadelphia Marathon, which also includes a half-marathon and shorter runs over a November weekend. The route takes in the National Historic District, museums along Benjamin Franklin Pkwy and Fairmount Park.

every part of Rodin's spectacular career include versions of *The Thinker* and *Burghers of Calais*.

The museum's small garden is always open and free.

Become a Brainiac at the Academy of Natural Sciences

MUSEUM

MAP: 3 P88 **F6**

The **Academy of Natural Sciences** (ansp.org, adult/child $27/23), the country's oldest natural history museum, has plenty of kid-pleasing exhibits, such as a hot and humid butterfly room with live specimens, and a terrific dinosaur exhibition where you can dig for fossils and bones. You can also watch scientists extracting fossils from stone. Other fun features include a drawing table where you can try your hand at illustrating insects, and delightful dioramas with exotic species set up in realistic poses in their habitats. At times, a giant animatronic T. rex guards the outside.

The museum was founded in 1812 and has been in this building since 1868. It's now part of Drexel University.

Get Lost in the Greenery at Fairmount Park

PARK

MAP: 5 P88 **B5**

The snaking Schuylkill River bisects this 2050-acre green space (myphillypark.org), the largest city park in the USA, splitting it into east and west sections. On either side of the river are cycling and jogging paths, playing fields, lawns, public art, and several historic mansions.

In East Fairmount Park, admire the Victorian-era rowing clubs at **Boathouse Row** (MAP: 6 P88 **B2**, boathouserow.org). Get a fine view from the terraces of the **Fairmount Waterworks** (p97), which is home to an excellent interpretive center on the city's water system and the park's natural environment.

West Fairmount Park was the site of the nation's Centennial Exposition in 1876. Memorial Hall, built for the expo, now houses the **Please Touch Museum** (p96). This section of the park also includes the 42-acre **Philadelphia Zoo** (MAP: 7 P88 **C6**, philadelphiazoo.org, adult/child from $25/20), the first in the country.

Find Zen at Shofuso Japanese House & Garden

GARDENS

MAP: 8 P88 **B6**

Built in Nagoya, Japan, in 1953 to a 17th-century design, the picturesque **Shofuso Japanese House & Garden** (japanphilly .org/shofuso, adult/child $14/9) was once part of a Museum of Modern Art exhibit in New York City but has been set in 1.2 acres of traditional Japanese gardens in Fairmount Park since 1958. Check online (japanphilly.org/programs/ program-calendar) for various events, including tea ceremonies, that take place here (reservations and extra payment required). Look up to see the incredible (and incredibly expensive) hinoki (Japanese cypress) wood roof, which was replaced at great expense in 1999 and 2010.

The cherry trees blooming in spring are not to be missed.

Tickets are timed and by reservation only. The house closes from mid-December to mid-March.

Survey the Scene from the Belmont Mansion

MUSEUM

MAP: 9 P88 **B5**

Get a panoramic view of the city skyline from the lawns surrounding the 18th-century **Belmont Mansion** (belmontmansion.org, tour $10). The mansion, administered by the American Women's Heritage Society, houses the Underground Railroad Museum, which tells the story of Cornelia Wells, a freed Black woman. However, it's frequently rented for weddings and events; call ahead to check (215-878-8844). Regardless of whether you can enter the building, the grounds are worth a stop.

Touch Everything at the Please Touch Museum

MUSEUM

MAP: 10 P88 **B6**

It's rare that a museum is truly hands-on, so the **Please Touch Museum** (pleasetouchmuseum. org, $22) comes as a refreshing reprieve for parents who've had to nag their kids to keep their hands off. Let your imaginations and your little ones run wild at this kid-friendly gold mine. Splash around while learning about bubbles and toy race cars, wander through a wonderland of trick mirrors and illusions, and ride a beautiful antique fairground carousel. Note the impressive arm of the Statue of Liberty made out of toys.

Memorial Hall is where the 1876 Centennial Exposition took place and is one of the few remaining buildings in the park from that

PHILADELPHIA TROLLEY WORKS & CARRIAGE CO

The city's largest tour company (phillytour.com) offers a variety of ways to see the city. Big Bus open-top double-decker bus tours, which you can hop on and off of during the 90-minute loop, and the motorized trolley tours are popular.

CHEERS TO PHILLY BEER WEEK

At the start of Philly Beer Week (phillylovesbeer.com), which actually runs for 10 days from late May into June, the Hammer of Glory – a custom keg hammer that's a symbol of Philadelphia beer – is used to open the week's inaugural keg with pomp and ceremony. Bars all over town run beer specials, put on trivia nights and host beer pong matches and other festive activities.

event. Its basement houses a scale model of the Exposition (costs extra). A floor renovation project is planned for 2026, which may affect visitors and traffic routes.

Get Pumped at the Fairmount Waterworks MUSEUM

MAP: 11 P88 C3

A National Historic Engineering Landmark, this beautiful Greek Revival complex (fairmountwaterworks.org, free) was built in 1815 and pumped water from the Schuylkill River until 1909. It was one of Philadelphia's biggest tourist attractions in its day and is still well worth a visit for its excellent interpretive center, where you can learn about the pumping station's history, the area's natural history, and the conservation of water resources and the environment.

See the website for guided tours of the center and around Fairmount Park.

Smile at the Froggies at Logan Square SQUARE

MAP: 12 P88 F6

One of the original squares from William Penn's town plan, it was named in honor of James Logan, an 18th-century mayor, and is centered on the Alexander Stirling Calder–designed Swann Memorial Fountain, with its large frogs and turtles eternally spouting water.

On the square's west side is **Aviator Park**, marked by the Aero Memorial and the All Wars Memorial, while on the east side is Sister Cities Park with a play area and cafe.

Welcome Spring at the Subaru Cherry Blossom Festival FESTIVAL

MAP: 13 P88 B5

Taking place over a week in early April when Philadelphia's cherry trees burst with blossoms, the **Subaru Cherry Blossom Festival** (japanphilly.org/programs/festivals/cherryblossom) celebrates traditional and contemporary Japanese culture with food, drinking, events and activities. The highlight is Sakura Sunday at Fairmount Park's Horticultural Center.

In addition to the events and cherry blossom trees at the nearby **Shofuso Japanese House and Garden** (p96), some Japanese restaurants throughout the city put on special menus.

Get Hands on with Science at the Franklin Institute MUSEUM

MAP: 14 P88 **E6**

You could easily spend the better part of the day touring this world-class science museum (fi.edu, adult/child $25/21). As well as being the venue for temporary blockbuster science exhibitions, it has a planetarium, IMAX movie theater and great permanent features, such as a giant two-story replica of a beating heart; kids can crawl through the arteries as if they were blood cells. Elsewhere, children can sprint and leap to measure their prowess and even watch dissections.

Benjamin Franklin founded the institute in 1824, and a memorial to him in the lobby includes a stunning 20ft-high marble statue in a rotunda modeled after the Pantheon in Rome.

MANAYUNK ARTS FESTIVAL

MAP: 17 P88 **B5**

Every June, hundreds of artists from around the nation set up shop for the two-day Manayunk Arts Festival, the region's largest outdoor juried arts event. Pieces from all mediums, from jewelry and ceramics to woodwork and sculptures, are available to peruse and purchase. It's a great way to pick up unique art pieces that strike your fancy and support artists.

Adore the Ornamentation of the Cathedral Basilica of Sts Peter & Paul CATHEDRAL

MAP: 15 P88 **F6**

The focus of Catholic life in Philadelphia is the gorgeously decorated **Cathedral Basilica of Sts Peter & Paul** (cathedralphila.org), dedicated in 1864 and enlarged in 1957. It's the oldest building on Logan Sq and was designed by Napoleon LeBrun and John Notman. The exterior includes a copper-covered dome and Palladian facade, the grandest of all Philadelphia's brownstone buildings.

The interior dazzles with murals, mosaics and stained glass, though the exterior is, by design, free of large windows. During the cathedral's construction, several anti-Catholicism movements were sweeping the country, and the architects adjusted their plans to make the structure harder to vandalize.

Watch the Thanksgiving Day Parade FESTIVAL

MAP: 16 P88 **E5**

Though New York City gets more airtime, Philadelphia also does a **Thanksgiving Day Parade** that's fun for all. Join the crowds celebrating the holiday and watching colorfully decorated floats, giant balloons of popular characters, marching bands in all their finery and uniformed first responders. The route goes along JFK Blvd and Benjamin Franklin Pkwy.

Check Out Artists' Studios During the Philadelphia Open Studio Tours

EVENT

Organized by the Center for Emerging Visual Artists, **Philadelphia Open Studio Tours** (cfeva.org/philaopenstudios) allows you to peek into artist studios in more than 20 Philadelphia neighborhoods and includes exhibitions, workshops, hands-on demos, artist talks and trolley tours. It takes place across two weekends in October.

Admire the Exterior of Cedar Grove

HISTORIC BUILDING

MAP: 19 P88 **B6**

This stunning house (closed at the time of research) is one of two historic structures in Fairmount Park managed by the **Philadelphia Museum of Art** (p90) (the other is Mount Pleasant). Cedar Grove was moved here from its original location in Frankford in 1928. Buried beneath various architectural additions, including a wrap-around porch and a 3rd-floor extension with a gambrel roof, is the original 18th-century summer house of gray native stone.

The interior can only be viewed on guided tours, except between November 30 and December 23 when the rooms are dressed for the holidays.

Join in Philadelphia Black Pride

FESTIVAL

Taking place over the same weekend as the **Penn Relays** (p141) in April, this multiday event (phillyblackpride.org) is on a mission to transform the lives of LGBTIQ+ people of color. Express your identity or show support at this festive show of pride by joining in the block parties, eating great food and making new friends.

PAVILION IN THE TREES

MAP: 18 P90 **B5**

If you're looking for a contemplative spot to ponder life and decompress in nature, stop at Pavilion in the Trees, a functional artwork by Martin Puryear tucked into a forested glade between the **Please Touch Museum** and the **Shofuso Japanese House & Garden**. A 60ft-long walkway raised 24ft off the ground leads to the pavilion, made from three types of wood, so it blends in harmoniously with the leafy surroundings.

Discover Art Exhibitions at the Perelman Building

MUSEUM

MAP: 20 P88 **D3**

Opening in 1927, the art deco **Perelman Building**, a branch of the **Philadelphia Museum of Art** (p90), houses small galleries devoted to special exhibitions of costumes, textiles, prints, drawings, photographs, and modern and contemporary design.

The building has an elaborately sculpted facade decorated with Egyptian-inspired reliefs.

LISTINGS

See p88 for map of locations

Best Places for...

$ Budget $$ Midrange $$$ Top End

Eating

Breakfast, Brunch & Lunch

Cosmic Cafe & Ciderhouse $$
21 B2
The view is the main course at this spot where you can order sandwiches and all-day breakfast plates and eat overlooking the river and **Boathouse Row** (p95). *8am-7pm*

Little Pete's $
22 D3
Come here for some of the finest Philly cheesesteaks in the city at reasonable prices in a spot near the **Museum of Art** (p90). *7am-9pm*

Sabrina's Cafe $

23 F5
This lovely little Philly mini-chain has several locations around the city. This one on Callowhill St has giant-sized breakfasts, friendly service and a homey, everyone-is-friends-here vibe. *8am-3pm*

Monkey & the Elephant $$
24 C1
This spot is special because it allows foster youth to work and gain valuable experience in the food industry. Great coffee and paninis. *7am-4pm Tue-Sun*

American & Mexican

Garden Restaurant $$
25 E5
Though expensive for the caliber of food, the service and setting are impeccable at the official cafe of the **Barnes Foundation** (p94). A great respite if you start suffering from art overload. *11am-3pm Thu-Sun*

Tela's Market & Kitchen $$
26 F3
A tasty place near **Eastern State Penitentiary** (p92) serving locally grown produce and excellent soups and sandwiches. It also has a grocery (pictured p102). *8am-3pm Mon & Tue, to 9pm Wed & Thu, 8am-10pm Fri & Sat, to 4pm Sun*

Cantina Feliz $

27 E3
Mexican favorites served in a cozy, casual, colorful spot with Day of the Dead murals and a nice outside patio. *4-9pm Mon-Thu, 3-10pm Fri, from noon Sat, noon-8pm Sun*

Greek

Moustaki Authentic Gyros $$
28 E6
Mouthwatering gyros, tzatziki, grilled meats and other Greek street food. Come hungry or plan on taking the leftovers back with you. *11am-9pm Sun-Thu, to 10pm Fri & Sat*

Zorba's Tavern $$
29 E3
This family-run spot has served authentic Greek specialties for decades, including fantastic hummus, excellent stuffed grape leaves, tender lamb and *saganaki* (flaming cheese). *11:30am-9:45pm Tue-Thu, to 10:45pm Fri & Sat, 12:30-9pm Sun*

Asian

Unit Su Vege $$

30 F4

It's hard to find vegan dim sum in Philly, but Unit Su Vege serves that and more in a clean, friendly spot near the neighborhood's museums. *11am-10pm Mon-Thu, to 10:30pm Fri & Sat, noon-10pm Sun*

Gyu-Kaku $$

31 F5

Huddle around a searingly hot grill for Japanese *yakiniku* (grilled meat), make your meaty selection and dip the morsels into a variety of sauces. *11:30am-10pm Sun-Thu, to 11pm Fri & Sat*

Kansai $$$

32 F4

Artfully presented sushi rolls, sashimi and nigiri at a small, clean and comfy spot near the **Rodin Museum** (p94). *11am-9:30pm Tue-Thu, to 10pm Fri, noon-10pm Sat, to 9:30pm Sun*

Fine Dining

Urban Farmer $$$

33 F6

More than 'just' a steakhouse, this fancy spot on Logan Sq offers fantastic farm-to-table meats and produce, all creatively prepared, and a selection of excellent cocktails and wines to pair with the meal. *7am-11:30pm*

Stir Restaurant $$$

34 C4

This fine-dining spot in the **Philadelphia Museum of Art** (p90) looks as beautiful as the pieces that surround it. It's open on Fridays for dinner. *11:30am-3pm Sat-Mon, to 8pm Fri*

Osteria $$$

35 H4

Elevated Italian dining in an elegant setting. The spacious glass-walled patio feels romantic and is the perfect complement to al dente pasta and delicious mains such as wild boar. *5-10pm Mon-Thu, from 4pm Fri & Sat, 4-9pm Sun*

Sweets & Desserts

Fairmount Flavors $

36 F3

Popular for frozen cakes, ice-cream sandwiches, cones and shakes, this deliciously sweet stop has everything you need to cool down – and most likely, a line out the door. *11am-11pm*

Federal Donuts & Chicken $

37 F6

Satisfy your cravings at this branch of the famous donut and chicken shop within easy reach of the **Philadelphia Museum of Art** (p90). *7am-8pm*

Drinking

Coffee

OCF Coffee House

38 E3

Across from the **Eastern State Penitentiary** (p92), this industrial-themed coffee shop can get you caffeinated and fed with a variety of veggie- and vegan-friendly food options. *7am-5pm Mon-Fri, from 7:30am Sat & Sun*

Twisted Grounds

39 F4

An out-of-the-way spot with excellent lattes, espresso and even puppuccinos (whipped cream for your dog). Proceeds go to help animals in need. *7am-4pm Mon-Fri, 7:30am-5pm Sat & Sun*

Peddler Coffee

40 E6

With pour-over coffee listed like fresh seafood at 'market price,' don't expect cheap, but the quality is excellent. *7am-5pm Mon-Fri, from 8am Sat & Sun*

Coffee Cream & Dreams

H3

Pick up some motivation and inspiration in addition to your cup of joe at this Black-owned business. There are lots of dream-themed quotes, as well as Philly-related souvenirs. *7am-1pm Mon-Fri, from 8am Sat & Sun*

Beer & Board Games

Crime & Punishment Brewing Co

C1

Discover your new favorite beer at this small, friendly brewery with a rotating selection. If you're having trouble deciding, the helpful staff make excellent suggestions. *3-10pm Mon-Fri, from 2pm Sat, 2-9pm Sun*

Thirsty Dice

43 **G3**

Philly's original board-game cafe, with hundreds of games to choose from. Have a drink and play them right there in the store. *4-10pm Tue-Thu, to midnight Fri, 11am-midnight Sat, to 7pm Sun*

Green Room

F4

A chill spot to grab a beer and shoot pool in a sports-bar environment. *3pm-2am Mon-Fri, from noon Sat & Sun*

Pubs & Dives

Kite & Key

F5

A great neighborhood bar with decent food, unique cocktails, a robust wine list and all the hop-laden favorites. *4pm-2am Mon, noon-2am Tue & Wed, 11:30am-2am Fri & Sat, 11am-2am Sun*

McCrossen's Tavern

46 **F4**

A fine Irish pub a short stumble from the **Rodin Museum** (p94), with excellent drink choices and food that's on the heavy side but fills you up. *noon-2am Mon-Fri, from 11am Sat & Sun*

Krupa's Tavern

 **C2**

Friendly dive bar that's simply a great spot to plop down, grab a frosty glass of beer and shoot the breeze with whoever is sitting next to you. You can even bring your own food. *4pm-2am Mon-Sat, from 1pm Sun*

Cocktails

Bar Hygge

48 **G3**

A beautiful bar and restaurant with innovative, creative cocktails and delightful wines that's worth checking out, especially if you're planning to visit the **Eastern State Penitentiary** (p92). *4-10pm Tue-Thu, to 11pm Fri, 10am-9pm Sat & Sun*

Assembly Rooftop Lounge

 **F6**

Toast to bird's-eye views of the **Cathedral Basilica of Sts Peter and Paul** (p98). Cocktails are tasty, but the view is the best reason to come here. *4-11pm Sun-Thu, to midnight Fri & Sat*

Shopping

Fashion & Accessories

Project HOMEspun Boutique

50 **H3**

Support people who are experiencing homelessness by shopping at this used clothing store that gives 100% of its proceeds to Project HOME, a Philly-based nonprofit that helps low-income folks get housing. *11am-6pm Mon-Sat*

New Style Ladies Shop

51 **C1**

This store is particularly known for its great hat selection, but you can also scour the selection for other accessories, from jewelry to shoes. *10am-6pm Mon-Sat*

Art & Books

Neighborhood Potters

 **F3**

This creative pottery studio and gallery opens its doors for a few hours each weekend if it doesn't have an exhibition on. *noon-4pm Sat*

Bookhaven

 **E3**

Purchase a new-to-you tome from this cluttered used bookstore piled with books at prices vastly better than buying new. *11am-7pm Wed-Fri, from noon Sat & Sun*

Book Corner

 **F5**

Find gently used or well-thumbed-through books. Try before you buy at this bookstore's nice reading area; it also has a friendly cat. *10am-6pm Mon-Sat*

Philadelphia Museum of Art Store

55 **C3**

It's hard to beat the quality and beauty of art-inspired gifts from the museum's store, from prints and lithographs to pens and coffee mugs. *10am-5pm Thu & Sat-Mon, to 8:45pm Fri*

Gifts & Souvenirs

Ali's Wagon

56 **F3**

This little spot across from the **Eastern State Penitentiary** (p92) is crammed with great gifts and souvenirs, from tees to pot holders, many with fun Philly phrases. *11am-6pm Mon-Fri, 10am-5pm Sat & Sun*

See p116
for eating,
drinking and
shopping
listings

Explore
Fishtown & Northern Liberties

This area is light on traditional sights but popular for eating, drinking, partying and shopping. Some of the world's best restaurants are here. It also has a nice scene down at the shores of the Delaware River, with parks, casinos and distilleries. Perhaps the most famous attraction is the Edgar Allan Poe house, where the macabre writer spent six of his happiest years penning some of his most successful stories.

The gentrification that started a couple of decades ago in the former manufacturing district of Northern Liberties has since spread to Fishtown and parts of Kensington.

Getting Around

Walk

Walking this entire area would be tough, but it's a dense district, and it's easy to walk the hot spots.

Bus

SEPTA buses 43 and 61 go along Spring Garden St; buses 5 and 25 are also useful north–south routes.

Subway

Useful Market-Frankford Line subway stations include Spring Garden, Girard, Berks and York-Dauphin. The Broad Street Line also has Spring Garden and Girard stations.

Trolley

Services run along Girard St from Frankford and Delaware.

THE BEST

Step into **RAIL PARK** (p112), 3 miles of decommissioned tracks

Admire the beauty of the **UKRAINIAN CATHOLIC CATHEDRAL** (p114)

Listen to tales and poems at the **EDGAR ALLAN POE NATIONAL HISTORIC SITE** (p110)

Learn about distilling at **PHILADELPHIA DISTILLING** (p113).

Rail Park (p112)

ROBERT K. CHIN/ALAMY STOCK PHOTO ©

Walk Fishtown

You can't throw a stone in Fishtown without hitting a great spot to hang out and sip a drink, whether it's a carefully crafted cocktail or a nice frosty beer. This walk takes you from greenery along the Delaware River to some of the area's finest spots. Always bar crawl responsibly.

START	END	LENGTH
Penn Treaty Park	El Bar	1.4 miles; 3 hours

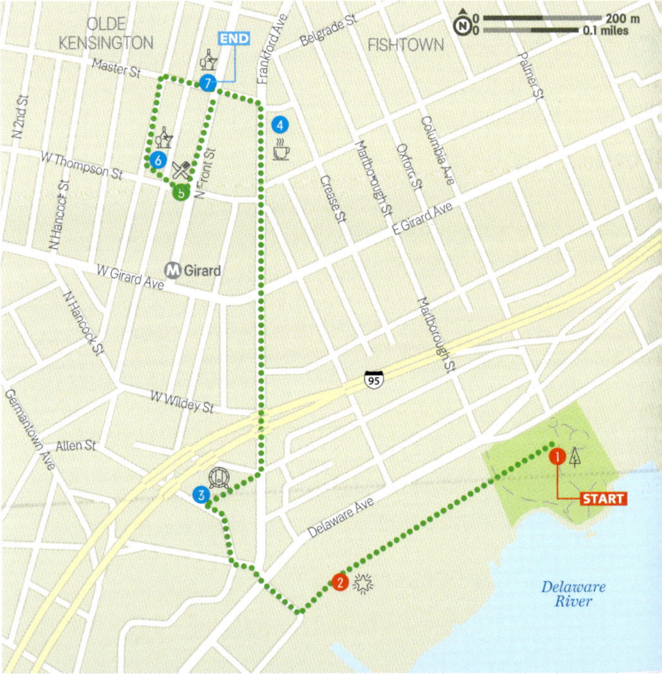

1 Park Life

Whether you're planning a ramble in the evening or during the day, start at **Penn Treaty Park** for fresh air, pretty views of the river and the sunset if you time it right.

2 As Luck Would Have It

If you're feeling lucky, step into **Rivers Casino**, roll the dice and perhaps walk away with some extra cash – or less of it. Even if you lose, it's a glitzy, glamorous spot to start a night out. The bar, not surprisingly, has built-in video slots you can play while boozing.

3 A Distillery by the Delaware

The old Ajax Metal warehouse near the Delaware riverfront has been revamped into **Philadelphia Distilling**, an impressive craft spirits operation with a sophisticated bar with craft beer and an inventive cocktail list. Learn about how these lovely liquids are made on a tour ($22 per person).

4 Coffee Cure

Follow Franklin St north until you find **La Colombe** on your right, the coffee shop's flagship location. This spot isn't the original store (the first one was near Rittenhouse Sq), but it's the current nexus, and lots of great coffee things happen here. Try the signature Draft Latte for a pick-me-up.

5 Laser Focus

If you're ready for some eats, stop at **Laser Wolf**, listed as one of the world's top restaurants in 2021 by Condé Nast Traveler. Reservations are a good idea (laserwolfphilly.com), though the bar might have open seats if you're lucky. Even if you don't fancy a full meal, snag a seat for a superb craft cocktail or two.

6 Kung Fu Fighting

A block away, the infamous **Kung Fu Necktie** bar is a spot where locals say 'you go to say you've gotten kicked out.' It's just a sometimes rowdy dive bar, but its compact size makes it a great spot for listening to live music.

7 Last Call

Finish your night at the always-packed, always-friendly **El Bar**, where beers are cheap and you can play pool or strike up conversations between karaoke sets. It's nothing swanky, but chances are you'll leave having had a good time.

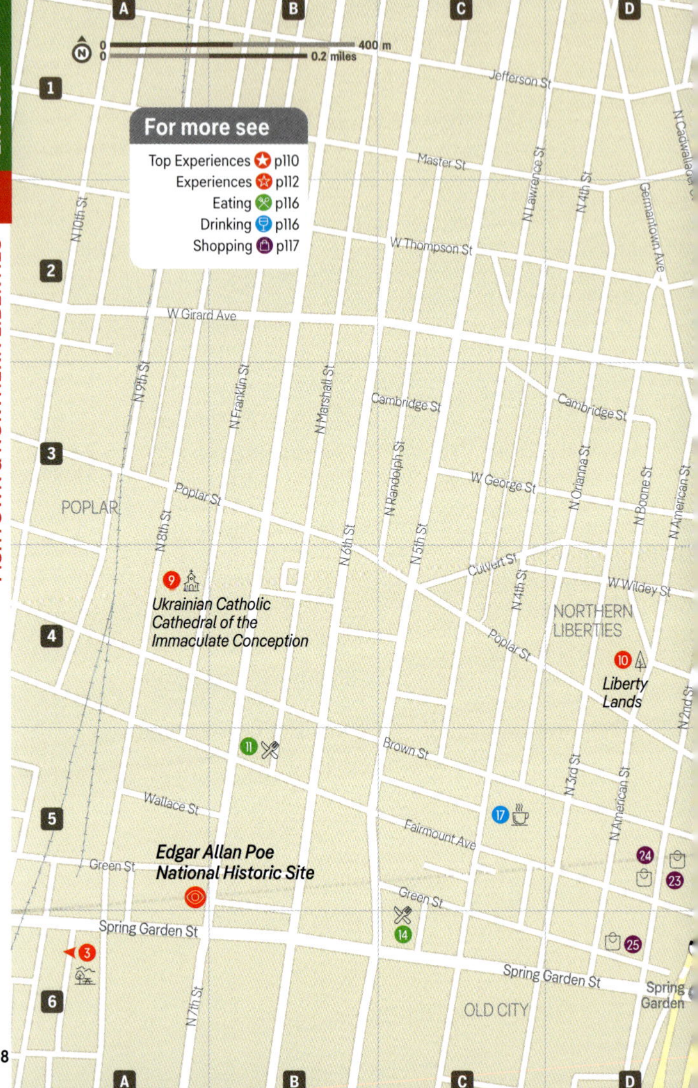
For more see
Top Experiences p110
Experiences p112
Eating p116
Drinking p116
Shopping p117
0 400 m
0 0.2 miles
A
B
C
D
1
2
3
4
5
6
Jefferson St
Master St
W Thompson St
W Girard Ave
Cambridge St
W George St
Poplar St
Culvert St
W Wildey St
Brown St
Wallace St
Fairmount Ave
Green St
Spring Garden St
N 10th St
N 9th St
N 8th St
N 7th St
N Franklin St
N Marshall St
N 6th St
N Randolph St
N 5th St
N 4th St
N Lawrence St
N Orianna St
N 3rd St
N Boone St
N American St
N 2nd St
N Cadwallader St
Germantown Ave
POPLAR
NORTHERN LIBERTIES
OLD CITY
Spring Garden
9
Ukrainian Catholic Cathedral of the Immaculate Conception
10
Liberty Lands
11
14
17
23
24
25
3
Edgar Allan Poe National Historic Site

E
F
G
H
OLDE KENSINGTON
W Oxford St
Palmer St
FISHTOWN
Belgrade St
Frankford Ave
N 2nd St
N Hancock St
N Front St
La Colombe
Marlborough St
Oxford St
Columbia Ave
Crease St
E Girard Ave
Girard
N Hancock St
Germantown Ave
Frankford Ave
Marlborough St
95
W Wildey St
Allen St
Fillmore
Philadelphia Distilling
Delaware Ave
Rivers Casino
Penn Treaty Park
Delaware River
N Front St
Columbus Blvd
1
2
3
4
5
6
1 2 4 5 6 7 8 12 13 15 16 18 19 20 21 22 26

★ TOP EXPERIENCE

Edgar Allan Poe National Historic Site

World-renowned for his creepy short stories, Edgar Allan Poe lived in Philadelphia in a house that's now a free-to-visit museum. The **Edgar Allan Poe National Historic Site** does an excellent job of shining a light on the troubled author's work and legacy.

MAP P108 **A5**

PLANNING TIP
Parking is limited, but it's only a 20-minute walk from Independence Park. Bus 43 stops at a nearby corner, and Indego bike-share stations are only a few minutes away.

Scan this QR code for opening hours

Brilliance, Genius & Demons

It's impossible to read Poe's macabre tales without wondering what the author's own life was like. Similar to his characters, Poe was a troubled soul. He was an orphan and had financial problems, his wife was gravely ill, and for much of his life, his literary genius wasn't appreciated. Poe struggled for many years, but Philadelphia proved to be a respite. He had a job editing a respected literary magazine, he wrote some of his most popular tales in this house, and he is credited with inventing the modern detective story. He died at 40 under mysterious circumstances in Baltimore, Maryland.

Don't Miss

The Edgar Allan Poe National Historic Site is a small museum, and it's easy to see it all, but don't miss the cellar, which may have been the inspiration for his short story *The Black Cat* and is where rangers occasionally do readings of the iconic tale.

Another top spot is the raven statue outside, an homage to Poe's famous poem of the same name. The garden has been planted with herbs and flowers that Poe describes in his works.

NATIONAL PARK SERVICE/VICTORIA STAUFFENBERG/PUBLIC DOMAIN ©

Creatives and readers should stop at the Reading Room, where you can bask in the ambiance Poe himself described in his essay 'The Philosophy of Furniture.'

Gift Shop

Edgar Allan Poe made a lasting mark on American literature and redefined what a short story should be. His talent for words brought lasting fame, though not fortune, at least while he was alive.

Pick up anthologies of his work in the museum bookstore, as well as cute souvenirs, T-shirts and even Poe bobblehead dolls. Rangers are happy to answer questions, and they are experts in all things Edgar Allan Poe.

QUICK BREAK

A block north on 7th St is the Fishtown branch of tasty Federal Donuts & Chicken, where donuts, coffee and fried chicken await.

EXPERIENCES

Get Messy at the Kensington Kinetic Sculpture Derby & Arts Festival

FESTIVAL

MAP: 1 P108 **G1**

Go wild and prepare for mud at the hilarious **Kensington Kinetic Sculpture Derby & Arts Festival** (kensingtonkineticarts.org), which takes place in early May. It features human-powered floats ranging from little more than bicycles to wildly extravagant creations, which do a 3-mile derby route through the area. Along the way, the creations must surmount various obstacles, including the Mud Pit, a massive pile of mud that must be traversed, often with comical fails, just before crossing the finish line.

This festival is the kind of crazy, fun-for-everyone event where the failures are as much fun as the successes. Enjoy lots of great music, vendors, food and shopping during the day. The event takes place rain or shine, so bring an umbrella (or just get wet).

Find Harbison's Iconic Milk Bottle

LANDMARK

MAP: 2 P108 **F1**

Boston has its famous Citgo sign, Hollywood has its hillside letters overlooking the city, and Fishtown has the **Harbison Milk Bottle**, an iconic water tower that has stood since the late 1800s advertising 'Harbison's Milk & Ice Cream.' A pioneer in the region's milk industry, Harbison's (with its trademark 'H') began producing milk before refrigeration and lasted for a century before closing in the 1960s.

The tower and buildings below fell into disrepair, but luckily the Historical Commission has preserved them, and the tower now has a fresh coat of paint and its cheery red letters of old.

Traverse Old Tracks at the Rail Park

PARK

MAP: 3 P108 **A6**

Rail Park (therailpark.org) is a grand experiment to turn an abandoned rail line into a multiuse public park with sitting and walking areas, performance spaces, and nice elevated views of the city. Phase 1 of this multi-decade project was completed in 2018, and it's a fun spot to bring a dog or walk with strollers or wheelchairs.

The long, narrow paths are nicely paved, and the route has been landscaped with broadleaf trees and flowering plants and bushes. If you're a yoga fan, check out the schedule of outdoor yoga classes on the Rail Park's website.

Catch a Show at the Fillmore

LIVE MUSIC

MAP: 4 P108 **F4**

The Fillmore (thefillmorephilly.com) is one of the top – if not the top – indoor music venues in Philadelphia, large enough to bring in lots of big names while still retaining an industrial and intimate feel. The building was once a factory, and much of the design today reflects that heritage, including original chimneys and reclaimed wood.

Something is happening almost nightly here, from comedy shows to live music. One feature that makes the venue popular is its open floor. Much like an outdoor venue, you're not confined to a particular seat and can weasel your way close to the stage (or arrive early and stake out space from the start). Recent stars to grace the stage include Jon Batiste and Margaret Cho.

Get a Taste of Philadelphia Distilling

DISTILLERY

MAP: 5 P108 F4

Philadelphia Distilling (philadelphiadistilling.com) offers not only great original alcohols, such as its signature Bluecoat Gin or Vieux Carre absinthe, but also tours of the facility, which are a fascinating peek into the way liquors are crafted. It's an entirely different process than making wine or beer, so even folks who've been to a microbrewery or two will find this refreshing and fun.

If you want to up your bar game, sign up for cocktail-making classes, which cover themes such as 'Cocktails 101' and 'Valentine's Cocktails.' While you're learning, you get to sample the tipples.

Kick Back at Penn Treaty Park

PARK

MAP: 6 P108 H4

Penn Treaty Park is often overlooked because it's not particularly large, but in some ways, that's why it's perfect. It's a great picnic spot or place to toss a Frisbee, with impressive river views that feature the **Benjamin Franklin Bridge**. The statue of William Penn reminds us that not all of his effigies are as large as the one on top of City Hall (p74) , and it commemorates the supposed place where a treaty was signed between Penn and the Native Lenape. Some historical debate surrounds the meeting and the treaty because the document vanished, perhaps as a way for Penn's offspring to nullify it and further disenfranchise the Lenape.

DRINKING & DINING AT SCHMIDT'S COMMONS

Schmidt's Commons has gone through many changes over the years and has had several different names. What was once the Schmidt's Beer building is now apartments, but the sign remains, overlooking the Piazza, named in honor of the Italian public squares. Bars and restaurants are springing up, especially along the Liberties Walk, a narrow pedestrian avenue that snakes through several buildings, making it a great spot for small groups or families with kids who might want to window-shop for their meal before settling into a venue.

THE LA COLOMBE STORY

Coffee shop **La Colombe** (MAP: 7 P110 **F2**; pictured) has its flagship shop in Fishtown, and this business is as much a Philadelphia success story as the movie *Rocky*. It features two guys with a vision who slowly but surely grew their coffee shop – at a time when only the big coffee chains had a corner on the market – from a small store in Rittenhouse to multiple locations around Philly and then all over the country. Stop in at this clean, beautifully decorated store for any type of coffee or espresso.

There are roses, flowering shrubs, some shade trees and a quiet ambiance. The paved paths are rough in spots but still usable with a wheelchair or stroller.

Get Lucky at Rivers Casino

CASINO

MAP: 8 P108 **G4**

Rivers Casino (riverscasino.com/philadelphia) is a fun spot to gamble and take your chances with Lady Luck. This casino has a wide array of options, from digital slots and 'one-arm bandits' to table games.

Many people skip gambling entirely and opt for a show or grab a bite, be it burgers, Asian food or a juicy steak. From upscale restaurants plating gourmet cuisine to casual eateries offering quick bites and comfort food, Rivers Casino serves something for every palate.

Admire the Architecture at Ukrainian Catholic Cathedral

CHURCH

MAP: 9 P108 **A4**

Beautiful and ornate inside and out, the **Ukrainian Catholic Cathedral of the Immaculate Conception** (ukrcathedral.com) offers an opportunity to steep yourself in cultural and religious heritage. The exterior showcases Byzantine and Romanesque architecture, adorned with intricate details and an iconic dome.

Inside, the sanctuary has colorful stained-glass windows, frescoes and icons depicting biblical scenes and saints. The iconostasis, a prominent feature, separates the sanctuary from the nave and is adorned with religious artwork. Witnessing a service allows visitors to experience vibrant Ukrainian Catholic traditions. Beyond the religious elements, the cathedral provides an opportunity to connect with the local Ukrainian community.

Escape the Hustle in Liberty Lands

PARK

MAP: 10 P108 **D4**

Liberty Lands offers an option for a serene escape, and this welcoming oasis is a nice respite if you've been doing a hefty amount of sightseeing. The gardens boast lush greenery, winding pathways and vibrant flower beds, providing a sense of tranquility even though the big city is just steps away.

Explore the diverse plants, relax on benches and enjoy a picnic on the lawns. Children can run amok in the playground or participate in activities during the frequent community events. Art installations and sculptures add to the garden's charm, and dedicated volunteers maintain it for all to enjoy.

NOLIBS

It sounds like something a partisan radio personality might say, but in Philadelphia, it means something different: Northern Liberties gets shortened to NoLibs. Founded in 1803, it was originally one of the largest cities in the country for half a century from the late 1700s to the mid-1800s until it was absorbed into Philadelphia. Settlers were allowed to craft their own rules hence the name. Northern Liberties is often called Philly's first suburb (though this honor is also claimed by a neighborhood in South Philly) and was the site for one of the country's most infamous red-light districts for decades.

LISTINGS

Best Places for...

See p108 for map of locations

$ Budget $$ Midrange $$$ Top End

Eating

Breakfast & Brunch

Federal Donuts & Chicken $

 B5

The Fishtown branch of this Philly staple has its usual crispy fried chicken and delectable donuts. Indulge in delights savory and sweet a short walk from the **Edgar Allan Poe house** (p110). *7am-6pm*

International

Suraya $$

 F1

Order lots of small Lebanese plates and other incredible Middle Eastern food such as *batata harra*, a spicy potato dish with cilantro and garlic, for an amazing and filling meal. *5-9:30pm Mon & Tue, 11am-2pm & 5-9:30pm Wed & Thu, to 10:30pm Fri, 10am-2pm & 5-10:30pm Sat, to 9:30pm Sun*

Pizza Brain $$

 G1

Serves inventive pizzas with a creative flair. With a vast array of toppings and a cozy atmosphere, it's a must-visit for pizza enthusiasts seeking unique flavors. *11:30am-8pm Sun-Wed, to 9pm Thu-Sat*

American

Silk City $$

 C6

This fixture on Spring Garden St since the 1950s still retains its diner-style chrome-edged bar, button seats and booth layout. *4-10pm Mon-Wed, to 11pm Thu, 4pm-2am Fri, from 11am Sat, 11am-10pm Sun*

Fine Dining

Laser Wolf $$$

15 F2

Delivers one of the neighborhood's top dining experiences, with bold flavors and expertly crafted Middle Eastern dishes. It's a restaurant from Israeli chef Michael Solomonov, one of his several great eateries around Philly. *5-10pm*

Elwood $$$

 F4

Unique farm-to-table Pennsylvania Dutch dishes, such as shad roe, are served on fine china. Also has high tea on weekends. *5-9:30pm Thu & Fri, 11am-2pm & 5-9:30pm Sat & Sun*

Drinking

Tea

Random Tea Room

 C5

With decor so eclectic it defies description, Random Tea Room has cozy nooks and a variety of tasty teas. Envision a Korean teahouse with a tea shop in Tolkien's Shire. *10am-5pm Thu-Sun*

Bars, Pubs & Dives

El Bar

 F2

Hopping spot with lively karaoke most nights, plus music performances, a pool table and inexpensive beers. *5pm-2am Mon, from noon Tue-Sun*

Frankford Hall

 F3

A massive beer garden with lots of German beers, plus ciders and nonalcoholic drinks, served indoors or outside. Food is nothing special, so stick to the drinks. *4-10pm Mon-Thu, 2pm-2am Fri, from noon Sat, noon-10pm Sun*

Kung Fu Necktie

 F2

This dive bar has a reputation, but that shouldn't stop you from getting a beer and listening to great live music. It's not a spot for a quiet conversation. Just get a drink and listen to the music. *7pm-midnight Sun-Thu, to 2am Fri & Sat*

Johnny Brenda's

 F3

A hub of Philly's indie-rock scene, this small venue has a balcony, a solid restaurant and a bar with equally indie-minded beers. *11am-2am*

Cocktails

Cedar Point Bar & Kitchen

 H1

A spacious bar, outdoor deck dining, good food and excellent creative cocktails make this a fun spot. The pickletinis are a huge hit, but the other drinks are just as artful. *noon-11pm Mon-Thu, to midnight Fri, 10am-11pm Sat, to 9pm Sun*

Rivers Casino

see 8 G4

This casino pours unique craft cocktails – try the Chambord Bramble with raspberry liqueur, gin, lemon juice and soda. Depending on where you go to sip them, you're right on the water. *24hr*

Philadelphia Distilling

see 5 F4

This distillery is more than just a spot to drink – you can also learn how to whip up your own great cocktails in its teaching lab. *4-10pm Thu, to 11pm Fri, 1-11pm Sat, to 9pm Sun*

Shopping

Crafts & Antiques

Architectural Antiques Exchange

23 D5

No suitcase is big enough for the architectural artifacts and one-off antique furnishings on sale here, but it's still fun to poke around the two floors of wares to see what's on offer. *10am-4pm Mon-Sat*

Casa Papel

24 D6

Apart from being a treasure trove of sheets in a variety of shades, textures and patterns, this colorful store also offers custom graphic design and specialty printing. *by appointment*

Fashion

RE Load

25 D6

Can't find your dream messenger bag in a store? Design your own at R E Load thanks to founders Ronnie and Ellie. Check out the brand's range of custom-made premium bags, as well as caps and wallets. *11am-6pm Mon-Thu*

Jinxed Fishtown

26 F2

Pick up retro clothing and interior decor at this cool jumble sale of a shop. *11am-6pm*

See p130
for eating,
drinking and
shopping
listings

Explore South Philadelphia

Sprawling, multicultural South Philadelphia appeals to visitors seeking diversity. A prime example is the historic South 9th Street Italian Market, the oldest outdoor market in the country. This area is a little hard-scrabble in some parts but gentrifying in others, so it will likely have something new next time you visit. This district covers Queen Village, home to Fabric Row; the hip gourmet strip of East Passyunk Ave; the repurposed Navy Yards; FDR Park; and the city's major sports stadiums. Quirky activities range from the Mummers Museum to Argentine tango studios. It's also home to some of the city's finest Philly cheesesteak spots.

Getting Around

Bicycle

Rent a bike using the Indego app (rideindego.com), picking up and dropping off all over South Philadelphia, such as the Italian Market.

Bus

SEPTA buses follow straight north-south routes through this district, making it easy to get around.

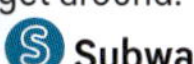

Subway

The Broad Street Line subway is useful for accessing the area. It stops between Lombard-South and AT&T (the end of the line).

THE BEST

Eat cannoli in Rocky's 'hood at the **SOUTH 9TH STREET ITALIAN MARKET** (p122).

Try on a costume at the **MUMMERS MUSEUM** (p124).

Attend a football game or concert at **LINCOLN FINANCIAL FIELD** (p124).

Admire the displays at the **AMERICAN SWEDISH HISTORICAL MUSEUM** (p124).

Navy Yard (p126)

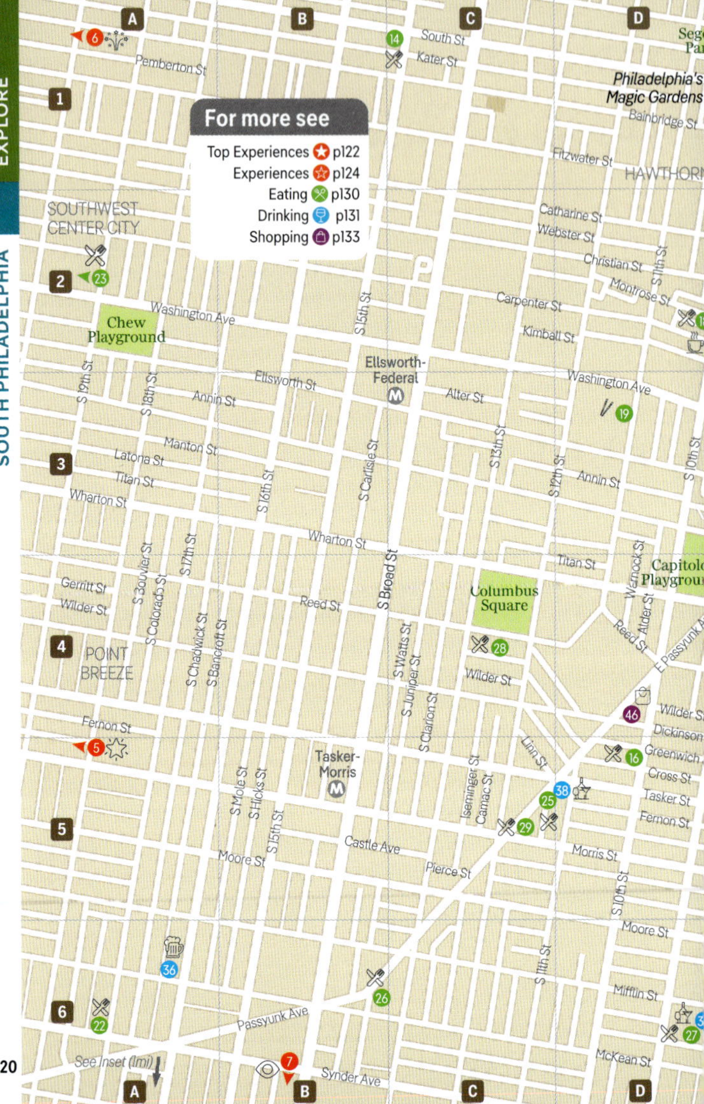

A
B
C
D
1
2
3
4
5
6
For more see
Top Experiences p122
Experiences p124
Eating p130
Drinking p131
Shopping p133
South St
Kater St
Pemberton St
Philadelphia's Magic Gardens
Bainbridge St
Fitzwater St
HAWTHORN
Catharine St
Webster St
Christian St
Montrose St
Carpenter St
Kimball St
SOUTHWEST CENTER CITY
Chew Playground
Washington Ave
Ellsworth-Federal
Ellsworth St
Annin St
Alter St
Manton St
Latona St
Titan St
Wharton St
S 19th St
S 18th St
S 16th St
S 15th St
S Carlisle St
S 13th St
S 12th St
S 11th St
S 10th St
Columbus Square
Capitol Playground
S Broad St
Reed St
Gerritt St
Wilder St
S Bouvier St
S Colorado St
S 17th St
S Chadwick St
S Bancroft St
POINT BREEZE
S Watts St
S Juniper St
S Clarion St
Wharock St
Alder St
E Passyunk Ave
Dickinson St
Greenwich St
Cross St
Tasker St
Fernon St
Linn St
Iseminger St
Camac St
Tasker-Morris
S Mole St
S Hicks St
Castle Ave
Moore St
Pierce St
Morris St
Mifflin St
McKean St
Passyunk Ave
Synder Ave
See Inset (1mi)

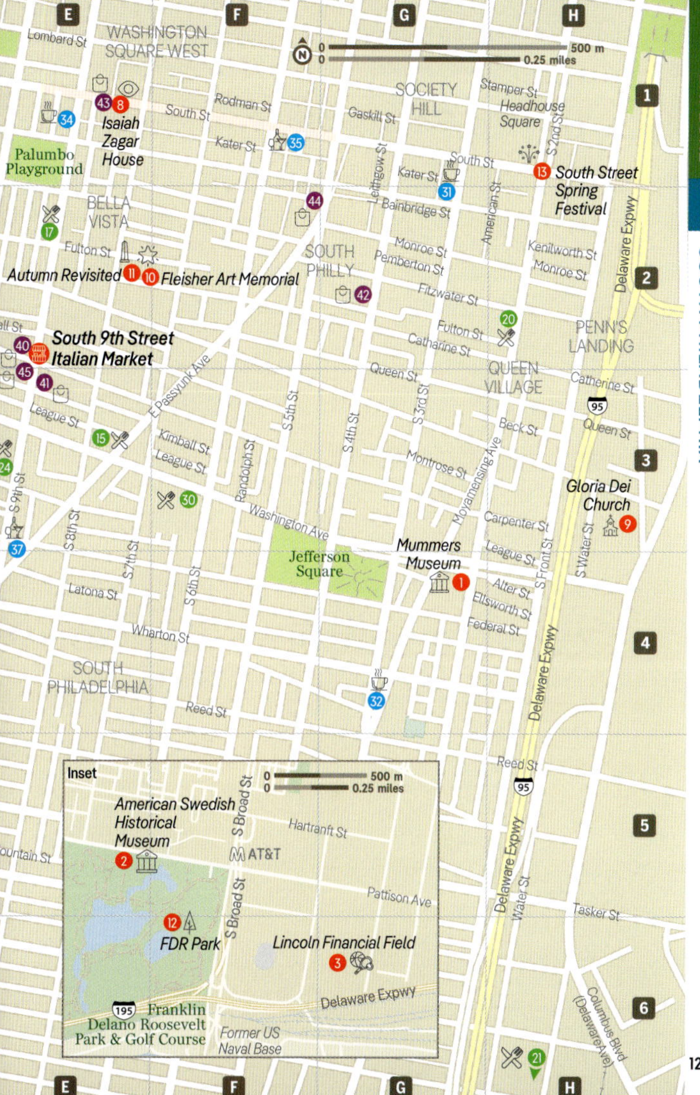
WASHINGTON SQUARE WEST
SOCIETY HILL
Headhouse Square
Isaiah Zagar House
Palumbo Playground
BELLA VISTA
SOUTH PHILLY
South Street Spring Festival
Autumn Revisited
Fleisher Art Memorial
South 9th Street Italian Market
PENN'S LANDING
QUEEN VILLAGE
Gloria Dei Church
Jefferson Square
Mummers Museum
SOUTH PHILADELPHIA
Inset
American Swedish Historical Museum
AT&T
FDR Park
Lincoln Financial Field
Franklin Delano Roosevelt Park & Golf Course
Former US Naval Base
500 m
0.25 miles

★ TOP EXPERIENCE

South 9th Street Italian Market

Head to the **South 9th Street Italian Market** to browse a long commercial strip lined with produce stalls, traditional butchers, fishmongers and delis over about 20 city blocks. The northern end is still predominantly Italian, while south of Washington St, more international shops are added to the mix.

MAP P120 **E2**

PLANNING TIP
Mondays are traditionally the day off for some vendors, but the market is still open, as are several of the shops.

Market History

In the late 19th century, Italian immigrants began settling in Philadelphia. They brought with them their culinary traditions, including a love of fresh produce, meats and cheeses.

As the Italian community grew, so did the market, which became a hub for locals to purchase authentic Italian ingredients and goods. The market's fame expanded in the 1970s when it gained national attention through movies like Rocky and Philadelphia. It's also expanded and now includes shops from around the world.

Popular Spots

The market is vast, covering 20-some blocks. Part of the fun is exploring without a plan. Alongside Italian, you'll find Mexican tortillas and Japanese sushi.

Di Bruno Bros Deli specializing in cheese, olives and charcuterie.
Cappuccio's Meats (p133) Butcher famed for its spirals of *chevalata* (a pork sausage made with provolone cheese and parsley).
Grassia's Sells spices and hot sauces.

Scan this QR code for a list of vendors and merchants

JEFFREY ISAAC GREENBERG 17+/ALAMY STOCK PHOTO ©

Cardenas Taste olive oils and balsamic vinegar.
Fante's Kitchen Shop Packed with all the kitchen gadgets of your dreams.
Talluto's (p133) Lots of authentic Italian pastas and sauces.
Sarcone's Bakery Great Italian sweets, breads and desserts.

Neighborhood Festival

Citizens in and around this strip throw the annual **South 9th Street Italian Market Festival**, a weekend party in mid-May that lays claim to being Philly's largest block party. Highlights include the Procession of Saints, a half-ball tournament (similar to baseball but played with a ball cut in half and a broomstick) and attempts at climbing a 30ft-tall pole greased with lard, with treats at the top.

QUICK BREAK

When you get hungry, stop at Ralph's Italian for a delicious, authentic and reasonably priced Italian meal. It's a cozy spot (read: often crowded) but worth the wait.

EXPERIENCES

Understand a Philly Tradition at the Mummers Museum MUSEUM

MAP: 1 P120 G4

Learn to tell your Fancy Brigades from your String Bands at the fun, colorful and curious **Mummers Museum** (mummersmuseum.org, admission by donation), devoted to the unique tradition of Philadelphia mummery, a flamboyant celebration that rings in the New Year. Reflecting the many immigrant cultures and traditions of settlers in the city, Mummers divisions famously parade down Broad St on New Year's Day in a bacchanal that rivals New Orleans' Mardi Gras.

At the museum, you can see – and not just on January 1 – many of the fabulous costumes worn over the years and even try some on while listening to Mummers music that would be played by marching bands. On Thursday evenings from May through September, the museum puts on free outdoor string band concerts and block parties starting at 8pm, and you might be able to learn the Mummers Strut dance steps. It also does kid-friendly events like brunch with the Easter bunny, so check the calendar for what's happening.

Admire Art & Architecture at the American Swedish Historical Museum MUSEUM

MAP: 2 P120 E5

Philadelphia's **American Swedish Historical Museum** (americanswedish.org, adult/child $15/5) is the oldest such institution in the USA, founded in 1926. Its handsome building, designed by Swedish-American architect John Nydén, is partly modeled after a 17th-century Swedish manor house and contains 12 gorgeous exhibition galleries. A highlight is the painted ceiling of the Grand Hall showing the Swedish arriving in the area (albeit with the cringe title of *Arrival of Civilization in the Delaware Valley*, which says a lot about the attitudes surrounding the painting and when it was created). The artwork is unequivocally stunning, and painter Christian von Schneidau also did murals on the walls. The museum also shows off beautifully crafted furniture, replica ships and photographs of famous Swedes who helped make Philadelphia what it is today.

It's just as pretty outside as it is inside, and the museum is a popular wedding venue, so you may have to plan your visit around a bunch of brides and grooms.

Cheer on the Eagles at Lincoln Financial Field STADIUM

MAP: 3 P120 G6

Lincoln Financial Field (lincolnfinancialfield.com), home of the Philadelphia Eagles, is a must-visit for sports fans. It's also the occasional stage for mega concerts, including Taylor Swift and U2.

Since the Eagles' 2018 Super Bowl win against the Patriots, it's become more difficult to get tickets to a game, but the determined can generally find a way. Plan as far ahead as you can to get tickets and prepare to empty your wallet – seats, or even just standing room, don't come cheap. Pray for good weather because the stadium is notorious for tunneling the wind.

Even if you're not here for a game, you can take a self-guided stadium tour (adult/child $15/10), usually on weekends but subject to the event schedule. Check the stadium website for the details.

Marvel at the Mosaics of Philadelphia's Magic Gardens PUBLIC ART

MAP: 4 P120 **D1**

The ongoing life's work of Philadelphia-based mosaic mural artist Isaiah Zagar, **Philadelphia's Magic Gardens** (phillymagicgardens.org, adult/child $15/8) is a folk-art wonderland of mirror mosaics, bottle walls and quirky sculpture that will mystify, mesmerize and perhaps even baffle. The art has an ethereal, psychedelic and almost cosmic element to it, as if you're seeing things that aren't quite from this world.

Zagar's mosaic murals can be seen around the city, but visit the Magic Gardens first so you know what to look for. This spot also puts on small exhibitions of other artists' work with a focus on those who are self-taught and making mosaics or folk art. Between November and March, site tours take place at 3pm on Saturdays and Sundays. Between April and October, walking tours around the area depart at 3pm Friday to Sunday.

Dance Argentine Style at Damian & Sarah Tango DANCING

MAP: 5 P120 **A5**

Tucked into a quiet residence in South Philly is **Damian & Sarah Tango** (damianandsarahtango.com), a wonderful studio run by a couple who've devoted their lives to performing and teaching this intoxicating form of dance. This isn't Buenos Aires, of course, but Philadelphia has a robust Argentine tango scene and is a fun place to give this beautiful art form a try.

ARMY-NAVY GAME

Marking the end of the college football season in early December, this traditional fixture sees the Army West Point Black Knights and the Navy Midshipmen from the US Naval Academy duke it out at Lincoln Financial Field. It's one of the country's most enduring sports rivalries, attended by some of the nation's highest brass, including the president. Philly is not the only place the game happens (in 2025, the match will be played in Baltimore before moving to New Jersey in 2026 and back to Philadelphia in 2027), but it's a good choice because of its location between the two academies.

Often called a dance that takes a lifetime to master, Argentine tango is essentially 'fancy walking,' so you may already have what it takes to begin – if you can walk, you can dance. Yet much like a language, Argentine tango takes practice and may take years to build up the 'vocabulary' for extended dances. Tango isn't a dance with memorized foot patterns; instead, it's a method where a leader learns to communicate to the follower, who in turn learns to listen for the leader's commands.

Damian & Sarah Tango offers instruction at all levels and can offer suggestions about where else to dance tango in Philadelphia.

Celebrate Black Culture at the Odunde Festival

FESTIVAL

MAP: 6 P120 **A1**

The **Odunde Festival** (odundefestival.org) is the largest street festival of its kind on the East Coast and by some measures the largest African American festival in the United States. Centered around South and 23rd Sts, this early June event starts with a spiritual procession to the Schuylkill River to mark the Yoruba New Year. Flowers and food are offered to the river goddess Oshun, and the ceremony draws enormous crowds.

In total, up to half a million come to party, watch dances and performances from big-name artists, eat great food, and make friends. Music fills the air, the streets fill with people, and the mood is a jubilant celebration. In addition to food and music, vendors sell African and African American products.

Check Out Decomissioned Ships at the Navy Yard

AREA

MAP: 7 P120 **B6**

From the time of the American Revolution until 1996, US Naval ships were built and repaired at the **Navy Yard** (navyyard.org). Although the Navy continues to house decommissioned vessels here, the site now functions as a business campus for companies such as GlaxoSmithKline and Urban Outfitters, whose headquarters stand in the shadow of the mammoth aircraft carrier USS *John F Kennedy*. Other vessels sit nearby in varying states of rusty, honorable decay. It's worth visiting

ATLAS OF TOMORROW

The subtitle of Candy Chang's interactive mural is 'a device for philosophical reflection,' and it embodies the idea of art as meditation and a tool for mental health. Beneath a monochrome image made up of more than 200,000 dots that were finger-painted by Chang and the local community is a giant dial. Though it no longer spins, it would land on one of 64 fables inspired by the I Ching that you can read for poetic guidance. It's at the corner of South and Juniper Sts.

Odunde Festival

for the ships alone, but the Navy Yard also has a great combination of historical and contemporary architecture, plus an attractive 4.5-acre park.

Landscape architect James Corner (of New York City High Line fame) designed **Central Green**, which includes a running track, ping-pong tables, hammocks and yellow Adirondack chairs. Beside the park is **1200 Intrepid**, a striking piece of contemporary architecture by Bjarke Ingels. The office building's angled concrete facade recalls both a giant wave and the bow of a ship.

See the Mosaic-Adorned Isaiah Zagar House

NOTABLE BUILDING

MAP: 8 P120 E1

Across South Philly, artist Isaiah Zagar has created scores of mosaic murals from found objects, discarded bottles, and bits of broken ceramic and mirror. The elaborately mosaic-covered **Isaiah Zagar House** at 826 South St was his first home in the neighborhood, a place he lived in as well as decorated. It began, as many art projects do, as a kind of therapy: Zagar had a mental health crisis, and exploring the art form of the mosaic enabled him to push through and reinvent himself. The works are

FRANK RIZZO MURAL IS NO MORE

For more than two decades, a giant mural of former police commissioner and mayor Frank Rizzo (in office from 1972 to 1980) overlooked the corner of Montrose and 9th Sts. It was regularly vandalized, a reflection of Rizzo's controversial legacy of police brutality and widening racial tensions. After the 2020 Black Lives Matter protests, Mural Arts, an agency that funds and maintains the city's murals, said it was severing ties and no longer paying for its cleanup. It was painted over that year, just days after a Rizzo statue was removed outside City Hall.

heavily inspired by his time spent as a Peace Corps volunteer in Peru.

The front door is painted with a gold self-portrait of Zagar with six arms standing above his mantra, 'Art is the center of the world.' It's now rented out as an Airbnb, but you can admire it from the outside. The interior is decorated with murals and mosaics as well.

The neighboring alley is also plastered with Zagar murals, while a block further west is the artist's ongoing masterwork Philadelphia's Magic Gardens (p125).

Visit the Gloria Dei Church

CHURCH

MAP: 9 P120 H3

Philadelphia's original settlers were Swedish Lutherans, and **Gloria Dei** (old-swedes.org) is the site of one of their first churches, built between 1698 and 1700. It's made of brick and was designed by English carpenters and masons. The simple, elegant interior of the chapel is notable for the models of the ships *Fogel Grip* and *Kalmar Nyckel*, which hang from the ceiling. These vessels brought a group of Swedes to the area in 1643, only a few decades after the *Mayflower* landed on Cape Cod, Massachusetts.

The church is photogenic from nearly any angle, but particularly so in the amber afternoon light when you also get the quaint cemetery in the foreground.

Read a Banned Book

LIBRARY

The Little Free Library project, in which members of the community exchange books through boxes in neighborhoods, has gone viral, and in Philly, it got a unique twist.

Little Free(dom) Libraries, marked with bright colors and found all over the city, offer readers the opportunity to discover a banned book, often by an author of color. It's a great way to find new writers or chat with kids about how important the freedom to read is. Find a list of locations at visitphilly.com/articles/philadelphia/little-freedom-library.

Harness Your Creativity at the Fleisher Art Memorial — ARTS CENTER

MAP: 10 P120 **E2**

A variety of classes and workshops take place at **Fleisher Art Memorial** (fleisher.org), founded in 1898. If you feel inspired to try ceramics or other art forms, this art school might be the spot.

Even if you're not feeling creative, parts of the building are worth a look because it includes the Romanesque Revival Episcopal Church of the Evangelist, designed by Frank Furness. The sanctuary features stained-glass windows by John La Farge, a mural by Robert Henri and an altarpiece on the life of Moses by Violet Oakley.

Samuel Fleisher, heir to a successful late-19th-century wool mill, founded the college as a means for the children of his factory workers to enjoy free art classes. That principle of making art accessible to all continues today. Classes book out as soon as registration starts.

While you're here, look for the beautiful mural called *Autumn Revisited* by David Guinn (MAP: 11 P120 E2).

Find Green Space at FDR Park — PARK

MAP: 12 P120 **F6**

The 340-acre **FDR Park** includes fields and lakes, making it the perfect spot to relax. Locals love to picnic here and use the facilities for boating, tennis, golf and sports.

The Anna C Verna playground opened in 2023, and it's a lot of fun for little ones, with sliding tubes, rope walkways and spiral staircases. Whether you're passing through or spending an afternoon, FDR Park is a delightful space.

Party at the South Street Spring Festival — FESTIVAL

MAP: 13 P120 **H1**

Not to be outdone by the Italian Market Festival (p123), South Street, aka the Headhouse District, comes alive with its own event in May. Spanning more than a dozen blocks along South St, this daytime festival and market showcase the area's restaurants, bars, and shops, featuring live music throughout.

In inclement weather, it is often postponed until October.

VIVID NEON AT ELECTRIC STREET

Los Angeles has Electric Ave, but Philadelphia has Electric Street, an otherwise unassuming alley with a nighttime surprise. Best visited at twilight, this installation is a collaborative work by mural artist David Guinn and light artist Drew Billiau, and has transformed a crime-ridden alley into a place of beauty. Though not intended as a permanent installation, there are no plans to remove it.

LISTINGS

Best Places for...

See p120 for map of locations

$ Budget $$ Midrange $$$ Top End

Eating

Breakfast & Brunch

Breakfast Den $$
14 C1
With breakfasts like 'Kale It What You Want,' you're sure to giggle as you read the menu. It's not just the fun atmosphere: the breakfasts are truly different from the normal fare. *8am-4pm Tue-Sun*

Cafe Diem $
15 E3
If you're looking for Vietnamese food and don't mind a crowd, stop at Cafe Diem for fantastic noodle soups and ice teas. Good for a healthy breakfast or light lunch. *8am-6:30pm*

Mexican

Blue Corn $
see South 9th Street Italian Market
An inexpensive spot where the presentation adds to the flavor. Blue corn tortillas are the go-to hit, but everything will make you feel like you've headed south for a while. *11am-9pm Mon-Thu, to 10pm Fri, 10:30am-10pm Sat, to 9pm Sun*

El Chingon $$

16 D5
A James Beard–nominated spot with fresh tacos and guac. It's a restaurant but feels more like a home. *11am-9pm Tue-Thu, to 10pm Fri, 10am-10pm Sat, to 9pm Sun*

Asian

Mawn Noodle House $

17 E2
Satisfy your cravings for Cambodian food, with spicy papaya salad and beef *saht koh* (skewers). *4:30-9pm Wed, 11am-2:30pm & 4:30-9pm Thu-Sat*

Tabachoy $$
18 D2
Filipino favorites like pork *sisig* (chopped meat with vinegar and spices) and *adobo* (a vinegar-soy combo) in a friendly spot that means 'chubby' (affectionately) in Tagalog. *5-9pm Wed-Sun*

Nam Phuong $

19 D3
This Little Vietnam spot boasts ample seating and generous portions in a casual Asian diner-type ambiance. Good for families and groups. *10am-9pm*

Royal Sushi & Izakaya $$
20 H2
A surprisingly authentic *izakaya* (Japanese pub serving tapas-style food), plus a reservations-only sushi bar, with hard-to-find-in-the-USA specialties, such as *agedashidōfu* (tofu fried with broth) and eggplant skewers with miso. *5-10pm Tue-Thu, to 11pm Fri & Sat*

Cheap Eats

John's Roast Pork $
21 H6
As casual as it gets, this Beard Award–winning cheesesteak spot is at a highway intersection. Cheery blue picnic tables await after you order. *10am-5pm Mon-Fri*

Stina Pizzeria BYOB $

More than just a pizza joint, this Mediterranean spot offers spanakopita, octopus, warm pita bread and pizza that's consistently rated as some of the best in the city. *noon-10pm Tue-Sat*

Porcos Porchetteria $

23 A2

Sandwich shop with excellently cooked pork, which says a lot in a city like Philly. This 'fast food' is made with care and serves a developing neighborhood, going head to head with big chains. *10am-6pm Wed-Sun*

South Philly Barbacoa $

A delightful stop for *barbacoa* (shredded meat, often beef) tacos and other Mexican delights. It's a small menu, but folks drive from the opposite end of the city to come here. *9am-4pm Fri & Mon, to 5pm Sat & Sun*

Fine Dining

Laurel $$$

Fancy French doesn't get much better than this, with surprising menu options like black onion poached cod and duck with knotweed. The desserts look as spiffy as they taste. *5-10pm Tue-Sat*

Le Virtù $$$

26 B6

Dedicated to the region of Abruzzo, this fancy Italian spot is impeccable. On Tuesdays, penny pinchers can BYOB. *5-10pm Mon-Thu, to 10:30pm Fri & Sat, 4-9:30pm Sun*

Sweets & Desserts

Machine Shop Bakery $$

With rough peeling paint and mint velour seats, Machine Shop is as fun to look at as the pastries are tasty. Focaccia and tender, flaky croissants are particular hits. *9am-2pm Thu-Sun*

Mighty Bread Company $

Get an order to go and escape the throng by eating in nearby Columbus Square Park. The orange ricotta teacake is spectacular. *8am-6pm Mon, Thu & Fri, from 9am Sat & Sun*

Kouklet Brazilian Bakehouse $

Bolo de rolo is the prime attraction at this Brazilian shop, which specializes in these tender, moist roll cakes decorated and flavored in a variety of ways. *10am-6pm Fri & Sat, to 4pm Sun*

Ba Le Bakery $

A Little Vietnam gem, this bakery has far more than just bread. Try the banh mi sandwiches, tasty fresh rolls and rice puddings. *8:30am-7:30pm*

Drinking

Coffee & Tea

Ox Coffee

31 G1

The heady smell of coffee hits you the moment you walk in the door. Welcoming, knowledgeable baristas make the drinks. *7:30am-1pm Mon-Fri, 8am-2pm Sat & Sun*

Herman's Coffee

Has the feel of a European corner store, with shelves of jams, jellies, and more. *6am-6pm Mon-Fri, from 7am Sat & Sun*

Tattooed Mom

Function Coffee Labs

33 D2

Unique twists on lattes, such as Cinnamon Toast Crunch and cardamom caramel, which might be why its name includes 'lab.' *7:30am-4pm*

Chapterhouse Cafe & Gallery

34 E1

A casual place with art installations and more than just coffee: sandwiches, milkshakes, muffins and spicy teas (turmeric and ginger mixes and lavender London Fog). *7am-10pm*

Bars & Dives

Tattooed Mom

35 F1

This iconic dive bar has great food, creative cocktails, an artsy vibe downstairs and crazy graffiti in the upstairs pool bar. Creative activities, such as occasional craft nights, spark conversation, and it's easy to make friends (pictured). *4-11pm Mon-Thu, noon-2am Fri & Sat, to 11pm Sun*

Second District Brewing

36 A6

Come for the great beer selection and stay for the old saloon vibe, with dark rafters overhead, a long laminated bar and stool seats. It's easy to have one beer turn into a few more. *noon-midnight*

Ray's 'Happy Birthday' Bar

37 E3

Come here for karaoke and to celebrate someone's birthday as if they were your best friend.

7am-2am Mon-Sat, from 9am Sun

Cocktails

Manatawny Still Works

 D5

It's pricier than many South Philly bars, but the cocktails are made with the shop's own spirits from its Pottstown distillery. *5-10pm Wed & Thu, to 11pm Fri, 2-11pm Sat, to 8pm Sun*

Bok Bar

 D6

Catch the sunset from this casual, picnic-style rooftop bar or enjoy an afternoon or evening outdoors with lots of fun events that liven up the beverage sipping. *5-11pm Wed & Thu, to midnight Fri, 2pm-midnight Sat & Sun May-Sep*

Shopping

Food

Talluto's

40 E2

A serious Italian Market stop for fresh-made pasta in a variety of flavors, plus olives, oils, pancetta and other Italian delicacies. *8:30am-5pm*

Cappuccio's Meats

41 E3

Everything you could want in a neighborhood butcher shop: a great selection of freshly cut meats and filled sausages served by staff who know what they're doing. *noon-5pm Mon, 8am-5pm Tue & Wed, to 6pm Thu, 7:30am-6pm Fri, from 7am Sat, 8am-3pm Sun*

Fashion

Moon + Arrow

 G2

As well as having its own jewelry line, this wonderful boutique sells a broad range of handmade and vintage goods to wear and for the home. It's a big supporter of local brands and hosts craft-related events. *11am-6pm Mon-Sat, to 5pm Sun*

P's & Q's

 E1

Specializing in excellent menswear, footwear and homewares, P's & Q's features sophisticated casual looks and timely contemporary fashions for men of any age. *noon-7pm Mon-Sat, to 6pm Sun*

Philadelphia AIDS Thrift

44 F2

Proceeds benefit organizations involved in the fight against HIV/AIDS, so you know your money's going to a good place. *11am-8pm Mon-Sat, to 7pm Sun*

Books & Records

Molly's Books & Records

45 E3

Secondhand records and books in mostly good condition, with a shop kitty to welcome you. *10am-6pm*

Philly Typewriter

46 D4

'The revolution will be typewritten' is the motto at this hipster goldmine that sells and services typewriters of yesteryear. *10am-5pm Tue-Fri, to 3pm Sat*

See p142
for eating,
drinking and
shopping
listings

Explore
University City & West Philadelphia

Across the Schuylkill River west of downtown Philly is the area that's home to both Drexel University and the Ivy League University of Pennsylvania (UPenn). Further west, toward Spruce Hill, are the green spaces of Woodlands cemetery, Clark Park and Bartram's Garden. The Schuylkill River makes for relaxing strolls and bike rides with lots of parks, playing fields and recreation areas. Delightful restaurants, bars, pubs, libraries, museums and historical monuments round out the experience of visiting University City and West Philadelphia, and it's all within an hour's walk of City Hall.

Getting Around

Bus

SEPTA buses crisscross the area, and two LUCY bus services shuttle in a loop around University City.

Subway & Trolley

Market-Frankford Line subway and trolley stations include 30th & 34th Sts. Trolleys also stop at 30th and 33rd Sts before lines split into north and south branches.

Bicycle

The Indego bike-share app (rideindego.com) lets you rent for an hour at a time, picking up and dropping off at numerous locations close to the main neighborhood sights.

Penn Museum (p140)
AUM CHAYER/ALAMY STOCK PHOTO ©

THE BEST

Dig into antiquity through archaeological treasures at the **PENN MUSEUM** (p140).

Catch the cutting edge of the art world at the **INSTITUTE OF CONTEMPORARY ART** (p140).

Be transported to the golden age of rail at the **30TH STREET STATION** (p139).

Discover horticultural specimens on a tour of historic **BARTRAM'S GARDEN** (p139).

WALKING TOUR

Walk University City

Home to the campuses of several universities, the area immediately west of the Schuylkill River is the academic center of Philadelphia. You can admire a broad range of architectural styles there, from Gothic Revival to contemporary, and creative pieces of art, as well as find tasty places to eat.

START	END	LENGTH
30th Street Station	34th Street Station	1.5 miles; 2 hours

1 All Aboard

While taking in the grandness of **30th Street Station**, with its enormous neoclassical hallway, marble-faced walls and 95ft-high coffered ceiling, check out the Pennsylvania Railroad WWII Memorial, a giant bronze winged figure also known as the Angel of Resurrection, at the east end of the building. In a room off the concourse's north side is Karl Bitter's sculptural frieze *Spirit of Transportation*.

2 Urban Greenery

Head south of the station to the Cira Centre South complex's parking garage. On its roof is a grassy 1.25-acre park called **Cira Green**. It's a pleasant spot to relax and offers splendid views of the Schuylkill River and the city skyline.

3 Glass & Steel

The striking interlocking glass buildings of the **Krishna P Singh Center for Nanotechnology** are set at angles and include a dramatic cantilevered box hanging three stories over the grassy courtyard. There, find Tony Smith's painted steel sculpture *We Lost*.

4 Nooks for Books

Architect Frank Furness designed the **Anne & Jerome Fisher Fine Arts Building**, UPenn's magnificent 1891 library. Clerestory windows and skylights light the catalog and reading room, which also sports a baronial fireplace.

5 Sculpture Park

The small **Blanche P Levy Park** is dotted with public art, including a *LOVE* sculpture by Robert Indiana. Locals like to joke that when the 1899 bronze of Benjamin Franklin sat down, a button from his vest popped off to create the giant white *Split Button*, a 1981 work by Claes Oldenburg.

6 Art Show

Andy Warhol had his first solo show at the **Institute of Contemporary Art** in 1965. It usually has two shows on at a time, but check the schedule (icaphila.org) because occasionally nothing is shown between installations.

7 Hair of the Dog

Drop into **White Dog Cafe** to admire this farm-to-table restaurant's quirky collection of canine-themed art. Wine and cocktails go for cheap during happy hour (4pm to 7pm weekdays).

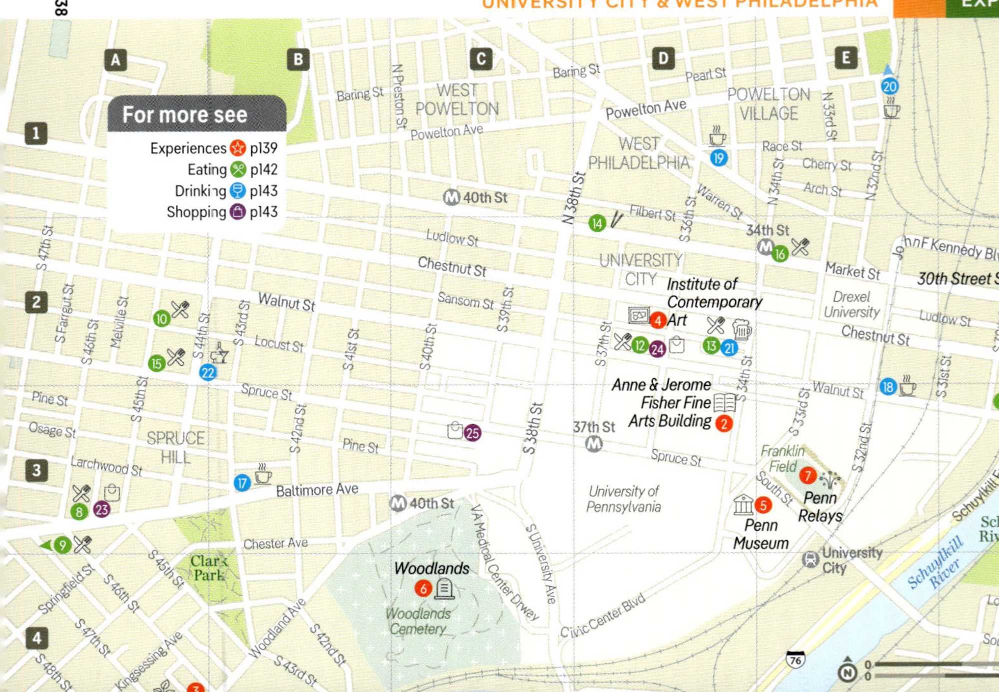
For more see
Experiences p139
Eating p142
Drinking p143
Shopping p143
30th Street Station
Institute of Contemporary Art
Anne & Jerome Fisher Fine Arts Building
Penn Museum
Penn Relays
Woodlands
Franklin Field
University of Pennsylvania
Drexel University
University City
WEST POWELTON
POWELTON VILLAGE
WEST PHILADELPHIA
UNIVERSITY CITY
SPRUCE HILL
FITLER SQUARE
Clark Park
Woodlands Cemetery
Schuylkill Banks
Schuylkill River Park
Schuylkill River
Schuylkill Expwy
30th St Station
40th St
34th St
37th St
30th St
Powelton Ave
Baring St
N Preston St
Pearl St
Race St
Cherry St
Arch St
Filbert St
Warren St
Market St
Ludlow St
Chestnut St
Sansom St
Walnut St
Locust St
Spruce St
Pine St
Osage St
Larchwood St
Baltimore Ave
Chester Ave
Woodland Ave
Kingsessing Ave
Springfield St
Civic Center Blvd
S University Ave
VA Medical Center Drwey
South St
Lombard St
Waverley St
Naudain St
N 38th St
N 33rd St
N 34th St
N 32nd St
S 47th St
S Farragut St
S 46th St
Melville St
S 45th St
S 44th St
S 43rd St
S 42nd St
S 41st St
S 40th St
S 39th St
S 38th St
S 37th St
S 36th St
S 34th St
S 33rd St
S 32nd St
S 31st St
S 30th St
S 25th St
S 24th St
S 48th St
500 m
0.25 miles

EXPERIENCES

Step into History at 30th Street Station

HISTORIC BUILDING

MAP: 1 P138 F2

Even if you're not catching a train, the grandness of the 1930s **30th Street Station** is worth seeing. The enormous neoclassical station's main concourse, with its marble-faced walls and 95ft-high coffered ceiling painted in red, gold and cream, is one of Philadelphia's most impressive public spaces. Corinthian columns support porte cochere (a roof over a driveway to shelter passengers getting out of vehicles) on the station's east and west sides.

The east end of the concourse is overlooked by a giant bronze statue, the *Pennsylvania Railroad WWII Memorial* (aka Angel of Resurrection), designed by Walter Hancock, who served in the US Army as one of the 'Monuments Men' who recovered art looted by the Nazis.

In a room off the concourse's north side, look for Karl Bitter's *Spirit of Transportation*, an 1895 sculptural frieze originally commissioned for the long-gone Broad St Station.

Get Schooled at the Anne & Jerome Fisher Fine Arts Building

LIBRARY

MAP: 2 P138 D3

Completed in 1891, the **Anne & Jerome Fisher Fine Arts Building** (library.upenn.edu/finearts), UPenn's magnificent library, is one of the finest examples of the work of architect Frank Furness, which is why it's also known as the Furness Building. The catalog and reading room is one of the most beautiful you will ever see, and it's a fun place to meander around and explore its nooks and crannies. Many of the windows have inspirational 'memes,' and you can ascend cool spiral staircases.

Exhibitions sometimes take place at the **Harvey & Irwin Kroiz Gallery** (9am to 4pm weekdays) in the building's basement. It also houses architectural archives.

You may have to work to find the small **Arthur Ross Gallery** (arthurrossgallery.org). It presents four to six different shows a year covering a variety of media. Exhibitions by famous artists, performances by musicians, and lectures by scholars and literati are the reasons to track it down.

Immerse Yourself in Nature at Bartram's Garden

GARDENS

MAP: 3 138 A4

Walking through **Bartram's Garden** (bartramsgarden.org, free), North America's oldest botanic garden, is a placid, pastoral diversion perfect for a balmy afternoon or sun-dappled morning. Founded by Quaker farmer John Bartram, the garden dates from 1728. The lovely 45-acre National Historic

Landmark, which includes the sturdy stone Bartram Hall and the Sankofa Community Farm, is open year-round.

Tours run Thursday through Sunday from April 1 to December 3. Garden tours are at 1pm and 3pm, and house tours are at noon and 2pm. Other activities and events that take place here include free kayaking and rowing on Saturday between 11am and 3pm from the end of April to the end of October.

When the Schuylkill River Trail bridges are completed in 2025, it will be possible to cycle, walk and jog directly from Center City to the garden. Check on the updates and find entry points at schuylkillbanks.org.

See a Show at the Institute of Contemporary Art

GALLERY

MAP: 4 P138 **D2**

Worth a stop if you're in the area, the **Institute of Contemporary Art** (icaphila.org, free) is where Andy Warhol had his first solo show in 1965. Other artists who have been exhibited include Laurie Anderson, Robert Mapplethorpe, Agnes Martin and Cy Twombly. The ICA usually hosts two exhibits at a time, from retrospectives to themed group shows. An impressive Virgil Marti chandelier hangs above the reception desk.

The gallery's exhibition spaces close, sometimes for weeks, between installations, so check in advance before visiting. It also has a library, shop and coffee bar.

Witness Ancient Artifacts at the Penn Museum

MUSEUM

MAP: 5 P138 **D3**

UPenn's magical **museum** (penn.museum, adult/child $18/13), the largest of its type in the USA, contains archaeological treasures from ancient Egypt, Mesopotamia, the Mayan world and more. One of the museum's most well-respected archaeologists, Dr Simon Martin, was instrumental in deciphering the Maya language and regularly offers lectures about the Maya world and discoveries in the field.

MARTIN LUTHER KING MURAL & MONUMENT

At the triangle intersection made by 40th St, Lancaster Ave and Haverford Ave, this memorial – consisting of a giant mural by Cliff Eubanks, a bronze bust of MLK by artist Rebecca Rose, and a historical marker – commemorates a visit by the famous preacher and Civil Rights leader to this spot on August 3, 1965, during his Freedom Now tour. The rally attracted a crowd of 10,000 people and was part of King's visits to cities across the country to thank his supporters. The mural depicts the leader with an upraised arm addressing a crowd filling the streets around him.

Stela 14 of Piedras Negras is a renowned work from the Maya that's part of the museum's collection.

Other highlights to look for include the granite sphinx of Ramses II, a dazzling headdress worn by Queen Puabi of Ur and colorful textiles from Hawaii.

The building itself is impressive too. Take a moment to admire its eclectic 19th-century architecture and design, which includes a Japanese gate, Arts and Crafts–style brickwork, a rotunda, public gardens, sculptures by Alexander Stirling Calder and a koi pond. The Stoner Courtyard is the location for a series of outdoor summer concerts.

Find a Famous Burial Ground at Woodlands CEMETERY

MAP: 6 P138 **C4**

A National Historic Landmark, **Woodlands** (woodlandsphila.org) is a 54-acre cemetery that was once the country seat of William Hamilton, who hailed from a family of wealthy colonial lawyers and politicians. Two of Hamilton's 18th-century buildings stand on the grounds surrounded by elaborate Victorian funerary monuments and shady trees he planted as part of his desire to craft an ideal English landscape. Many of Philadelphia's notable figures are buried here, including the artist Thomas Eakins and the surgeon Samuel David Gross, whom Eakins famously painted in *The Gross Clinic*.

Watch Runners at the Penn Relays EVENT

MAP: 7 P138 **E3**

Taking place over three days at the end of April, **Penn Relays** (pennrelays.com) is the largest and oldest track-and-field meet in the USA, with more than 20,000 participants from across the country as well as overseas. High school and college events pack the UPenn stadiums, and in a sports-loving state like Pennsylvania, it's a festive, thrilling and fun time for participants and spectators.

It's a rain-or-shine event, but umbrellas are not permitted, so bring wet-weather gear if the forecast doesn't cooperate.

LISTINGS

Best Places for...

See p138 for map of locations

$ Budget $$ Midrange $$$ Top End

Eating

Breakfast

Renata's Kitchen $
8 A3
Delightful spot with Middle Eastern food as well as American standards. Try the *shakshuka* (poached eggs with Moroccan salsa), the Moroccan carrots or one of the creative mocktails. *10am-10pm Tue-Sat, to 4pm Sun*

Cedar Park Cafe $$
9 A3
This casual joint dishes up hearty omelets, pancakes, hash browns and ever-popular fried chicken. *7am-1:30pm Mon-Fri, to 2:30pm Sat & Sun*

Lunch

Abyssinia $$

10 A2
A farm-to-table Ethiopian experience with lots of creative lentil dishes, spiced meats and vegetarian options, as well as two bars. *10am-2am Mon-Thu, to 9:30pm Fri, 9am-9:30pm Sat, to 8pm Sun*

Walnut Street Cafe $$
11 F3
This elegant, airy spot is great for breakfast, brunch and lunch. The food is haute American, with hot honey biscuits, fried chicken, and a fun 'mimosa kit' for you to mix the juice and champagne to your taste. *8am-9pm Tue-Thu, to 10pm Fri, 9am-10pm Sat, to 3pm Sun*

Louie Louie $$

12 D2
A bit fancier than some other neighborhood options, this place has a cozy fireplace and French cuisine. Try the pork belly croque monsieur. *11am-9pm Mon-Thu, to 9:30pm Fri, 10am-9:30pm Sat, to 8pm Sun*

Dinner

White Dog Cafe $$
13 D2
This cafe's really gone to the dogs – the white dogs that is, as evidenced by the dog-related ceramic kitsch, paintings and pillows. The food is a cut above, with creatively prepared farm-to-table dishes. *11am-9pm*

Han Dynasty $$
14 D2
This west-side outpost of the local mini-empire offers sizzling Sichuan goodness. It's a shed-like space with some communal shared tables – perfect for large groups of hungry student diners. *11:30am-9:30pm Sun-Thu, to 10pm Fri & Sat*

Don Barriga $

15 A2
Cheap, cheery and colorful, both in decor and in the plating, Don Barriga has authentic Mexican tacos, salsas and guacamoles made using locally sourced ingredients when possible. *10am-10pm Mon-Sat, to 9pm Sun*

Landmark Americana Tap & Grill $$

16 E2
A pub with better grub than most. Come for standbys like 'I Dare You' buffalo wings (spicy!), jerk salmon or the grain bowl. *11am-midnight Sun-Wed, to 1am Thu-Sat*

Drinking

Coffee

Green Line Cafe

 B3

A popular spot named after the trolley line that passes outside. It's a relaxed place to linger over organic drip coffee, loose-leaf tea or vegan soup, or you can get your order to go and enjoy it across the road in Clark Park. *7am-6pm Mon-Sat, from 8am Sun*

Top Hat Coffee Lounge

 E3

A rarity with coffee shops these days: ample seating! Plus great drip, brewed and espresso options. The waffles are highly recommended. *7am-3pm Mon-Fri, 9am-4pm Sat & Sun*

Madis Coffee

 D1

The crema on these espressos rivals the head on a pour of Guinness. This space is clean and friendly and has outdoor seating. *7am-6pm Mon-Fri, from 8am Sat & Sun*

Arterial Coffee

 E1

Look for the dragonfly logo to find this bright and airy spot with fresh danishes, avocado smash toast and excellent coffee. *7am-4pm Mon-Fri, from 8am Sat & Sun*

Pubs & Dives

New Deck Tavern

 D2

An Irish pub that could easily be the set for *How I Met Your Mother*, New Deck Tavern has great pours, a rounded menu of bar food and burgers, and outdoor seating. *11am-midnight Tue & Wed, to 1am Thu-Sun*

Fiume

see  A2

Upstairs at **Abyssinia** (p142), this crowded dive bar always has a friendly vibe with a good selection of beer and wacky craft cocktails. *6pm-12:30am*

Local 44

 B2

Not just a great spot to down a beer or cocktail, Local 44 also has vegan and vegetarian bar food options, such as buffalo seitan wings. *4-11pm Mon-Thu, noon-midnight Fri, from 11am Sat & Sun*

Shopping

Fashion & Books

Jinxed West Philly

23 A3

One of Philly's best vintage stores offers up a keenly edited and photogenic selection of homewares and decorative retro items, including posters, paintings, photos, rugs and clothing. *11am-6pm*

Penn Bookstore

24 D2

The massive Penn Bookstore is your go-to spot for sports and university apparel, as well as cups, mugs, pennants and all things UPenn. *8:30am-8pm Mon-Fri, from 10am Sat, 10am-6pm Sun*

House of Our Own

25 C3

Books, new and secondhand, covering topics from addiction to zoology, are piled high and wide across the two floors of this bookshop in a Victorian mansion squished between the frat houses of University City. *11am-6pm Mon-Fri, from noon Sat & Sun*

TURO
Skip the rental counter
Train Information
11:03 am
Messaging
Attention please. This is the last call for New Jersey Transit 4623 en route to Atlantic City, with intermediate stops. Passengers should proceed to Gate 10 Track 10.
RED CAP

Philadelphia Toolkit

30th Street Station (p139)

BRYAN LITTEL/SHUTTERSTOCK ©

Family Travel

Philly is a traveling family's dream, with ample playgrounds, parks, zoos and kid-friendly museums to suit just about any toddler-to-teen needs. Families of all types and stripes will have a blast here.

Is Philadelphia Good for Kids?

In a word, yes! This city has so much to do, see and experience that kids – and parents – find Philly a fun place. Seek out historical monuments, museums and science-related spots where kids can see and learn about the people and places they may have already heard about in history books.

PARKS & PLAYGROUNDS

Philadelphia has hundreds of parks and playgrounds within its boundaries, many with jungle gyms and slides, and others with sculptures and fountains.

Scan the QR code for a Philadelphia Parks & Recreation map:

Dining Out

While many restaurants are swanky, few – if any – turn away well-behaved children. Numerous inexpensive kid-friendly dining options range from family-oriented chains to family-run Chinatown restaurants and Italian places that welcome you with the-more-the-merrier hospitality. Most restaurants have kids menus, and all but the fanciest have a high chair or two.

Travel with Children

Some museums are made for kids, while others, such as Eastern State Penitentiary and the Mütter Museum, may be extreme for youngsters.

Public Transport

Children under age 12 who are accompanied by a fare-paying adult ride for free on SEPTA.

Admission Fees

Some museums offer free entry right up to age 18, but most have a cutoff at ages 5 or 12. Discounts for youth and seniors are common, often at ages 12 and 55 respectively.

Accommodations

Philly has lots of options to fit most budgets, but overall, it isn't a cheap city to stay in.

Where to Stay if You Love...

Nightlife & Street Art

Chinatown & the Gayborhood (p53) Everywhere's a good place to drink and be merry, but these neighborhoods are particularly great spots, with plenty to see and do.

Architecture & Shopping

Rittenhouse Square & City Center West (p69) Staying close to City Hall gives you walking access to the art museums. This swanky neighborhood also has fashionable shops.

OUR PICK

We Love to Stay In...

Rittenhouse Square & City Center West (p69). This 'hood has so much to see and do, from the stately Rittenhouse Sq to the secret speakeasies on Sansom St, plus lots of great restaurants in a surprising range of options that fit almost all budgets, all within a block or two from the square. In spring, Rittenhouse Square is especially pretty.

Food & Drink

Fishtown & Northern Liberties (p105) Breweries, distilleries, restaurants and artists' studios are popping up in this former manufacturing district.

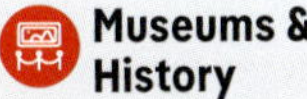

Museums & History

Old City & Society Hill (p31) History buffs love staying near the dozens of impressive museums that stand as a testament to the country's founding fathers.

Art & Culture

South Philly (p119) With its Italian Market, Little Vietnam and tango studio, this melting pot makes a good spot for the culturally curious to spend the night.

HOW MUCH FOR A NIGHT IN A

Hostel dorm bed from **$35**

Boutique midrange hotel from **$150**

Centrally located hotel from **$250**

Food, Drink & Nightlife

Allergies & Intolerances

Generally, restaurants are happy to cater to special dietary needs, but you may not find the full information listed in detail on the menu. If you have a serious allergy or specific requirements, contact the restaurant in advance to find out how carefully it can cater to your needs.

ONLY IN PHILLY

Citywide Special
A shot (usually Jim Beam whiskey) and a cheap beer (often PBR).

Philly Taco
A Philly cheesesteak wrapped in slices of pizza.

Wooder Ice
The Philly way to pronounce 'water ice' (aka shave ice), an Italian specialty.

A LIVING WAGE

An increasing number of restaurants add a tip of 18% or more to the tab automatically to ensure that the servers and other staff earn enough to pay their bills and make ends meet. You're not required to tip additionally, but any extra you wish to offer is always greatly appreciated.

Cheesesteaks

When you order a famous Philly cheesesteak, say the type of cheese (American, provolone or 'whiz,' cheese in a can that's sprayed like whipped cream) and 'wit' or without onions. For example, 'Whiz wit' translates to 'a cheesesteak with Cheese Whiz and onions.' A 'provo-lone' has provolone cheese and omits the onions.

HOW TO... Pay the Bill

You may be presented with the bill without asking for it, but that's not usually a signal you have to leave.

Splitting the bill If you need to split the bill of a larger group, make sure the server knows in advance. If it's just a simple one, like 50/50 and two cards, that's usually not a problem to mention later.

Tipping Tipping some amount is required, even for lackluster service or a bad meal. For a meal you like, consider 18% to 25%. Often, an 18% tip for groups of six or more is added automatically.

PRICE RANGES

The following price ranges refer to the average cost of a main course.

$ less than $15

$$ $15–35

$$$ more than $35

OPENING HOURS

Cafes 7am to 3pm

Restaurants 11am to 10pm; some offer a limited menu until midnight

Bars 6pm to midnight or later

Going Out

Dive bars Plan on a night of cheap beer, playing pool and picking out your favorite tunes from the jukebox at these inexpensive, often plain or even shabby watering holes that are often the everybody-knows-your-name type of joint.

Speakeasies Philly has a few of these swanky, high-class bars. Generally, you need to wait in line (sometimes for hours) just to put your name on the list. Once your seat is ready, you get a text and have a limited amount of time to get back to the venue or else forfeit your spot.

Nightclubs Philadelphia's nightclub scene is generally relaxed, though you may need to wait in line on popular nights. Don't show up plastered, and don't give the bouncers a reason to turn you away, such as talking smack. A valid ID is required, even if you're 80 years old.

HOW MUCH FOR A

Soft pretzel $1–2

Domestic beer $3–5

Craft beer $5–7

Coffee $4–7

Standard cocktail $10

Craft cocktail $15

Wooder Ice $3–5

LGBTIQ+ Travelers

Philly is a proud city, and LGBTIQ+ travelers will feel welcomed not only in the Gayborhood but also across the city.

The Gayborhood

Marked with bright rainbow crosswalks and countless flags, the Gayborhood is a district bounded by Chestnut and Pine on the north and south and Broad and 11th to the east and west. However, Philadelphia is home to many LGBTIQ-friendly and -owned venues outside this district.

Thankfully, Philadelphia has little crime directed toward the LGBTIQ+ population. Gay and lesbian couples are treated with the same dignity and respect as straight couples. Two men traveling together are likely to be assumed to be a couple, even if they're just buddies sharing a room to keep costs down.

Don't miss **Philly Pride**. The entire city celebrates, and the festivities and parade are legendary. While the Gayborhood is often the main attraction, travelers can find plenty of LGBTIQ-owned, -operated or -friendly establishments throughout the city.

OUR PICKS

What to Look For

DRAG SHOWS If you haven't seen a drag show, Philly is just the spot for it.

KARAOKE NIGHTS Belt out crowd-favorite tunes.

DANCE PARTIES Clubs host themed nights with lots of costumes.

Look for discussions, movie screenings and lectures.

HAPPY HOUR Gayborhood happy-hour specials and themed drink nights happen throughout the week.

PRIDE

Tens of thousands take part in this gala event in June, when the streets flood with rainbows and people from all walks of life join together to celebrate Pride.

GAYBORHOOD TOURS

Hear quirky and queer fun facts on a Gayborhood and LGBTQ History tour with Beyond The Bell.

Resources

• **Visit Philly** (visitphilly.com/lgbt) See the latest events and get suggestions for things to see and do. • **William Way Community Center** This inclusive organization has events and resources for those in the LGBTIQ+ community.

Health & Safe Travel

Philadelphia has a reputation as a tough, gritty city, but if you're aware of your surroundings, it's unlikely you'll have problems.

TAP WATER

Philadelphia's tap water is perfectly safe to drink, so bringing a reusable bottle is highly recommended. Tap water at restaurants is free, but bottled water is charged for.

Marijuana

Unlike in many other states, marijuana (cannabis) is not legal in Pennsylvania. However, the possession of small amounts of pot has been decriminalized inside Philadelphia proper (not its neighboring regions). As in many parts of the world, seeking out illegal substances may turn a great vacation into a bad one quickly, so you're safest leaving the 'recreation' for another time.

Transport

Driving or cycling under the influence and fare-dodging on public transport are punishable offenses.

Health Insurance

Hospitals in the USA are expensive, and insurance is a hellscape of bureaucratic red tape. That said, federal law requires hospitals to administer emergency treatment regardless of your ability to pay. The definition of 'emergency,' however, can be a matter of opinion, so your best option is to have comprehensive travel insurance that covers emergency visits and unexpected health concerns.

QUICK INFO

Streets

Be aware of your surroundings while walking late at night.

Hotels

Check fire exits and use the security locks on your doors.

Marijuana & Tobacco

Though marijuana is decriminalized, smoking or vaping in a hotel means a hefty fine.

Responsible Travel

Follow these tips to leave a lighter footprint, support local and have a positive impact on communities.

Indego Bike Sharing

Cycling is a great way to get around town without a carbon footprint, and Philly's Indego bike-sharing app (rideindego.com) lets you take advantage of the city's fleet.

The basic fee of $15 gets you 24 hours of unlimited bike use as long as you ride for an hour or less each time. Once you dock the bike, you can check it out again for another hour-long period.

Recycling

Philadelphia is behind the curve when it comes to recycling. While many cities have multiple bins to separate plastics, paper and food waste, the attitude here is to chuck it.

OUR PICK

Deals on Day-Old

If you don't need the freshest donuts, pretzels or bagels, look for the day-olds, which are super cheap. You're helping reduce waste and saving money at the same time.

Reusable Water Bottles

Increasingly, plastics are finding their way into even the most remote places, and reducing plastic use helps the planet. Reusable water bottles are easy to refill at many places around the city, such as hotel lobbies and restaurants. Bringing a reusable cup to coffee shops helps too.

Resources

- phila.gov Great for bike maps and info on navigating the city's public transport system.
- visitphilly.com Information, advice and downloadable maps.

FROM LEFT: EQROY/SHUTTERSTOCK ©, BECKY STARSMORE/SHUTTERSTOCK ©

CLIMATE CHANGE

Like many major cities, Philadelphia is experiencing more extreme weather. Be aware of travel alerts should there be an emergency. Text 888-777 or sign up at ReadyPhiladelphia (phila.gov/departments/oem/programs/readyphiladelphia) to get alerts on your phone or by email.

Secondhand Stores

Shopping at secondhand stores is a great way to reduce waste and reuse. By buying secondhand, you're effectively dropping the shipping costs of the purchased item to zero. By wearing it longer, your wardrobe addition hasn't harmed the planet. **Philly AIDS Thrift** is a great spot to get deals on second-hand clothing, and your purchase helps those affected by HIV/AIDS. LGBTIQ-owned **Charli Vintage & Thrift** is another spot to check out, with a stylish selection of mostly vintage clothes.

PHILLY BIKE MAP

Scan this QR code for a bike-friendly map of the city. It also lists Indego bike-share locations and what to do in case of theft or accidents.

Climate Change & Travel

It's impossible to ignore the impact we have when travelling; Lonely Planet urges all travellers to engage with their travel carbon footprint, which will mainly come from air travel. While there often isn't an alternative, travellers can look to minimise the number of flights they take, opt for newer aircrafts and use cleaner ground transport, such as trains. One proposed solution—purchasing carbon offsets—unfortunately does not cancel out the impact of individual flights. While most destinations will depend on air travel for the foreseeable future, for now, pursuing ground-based travel where possible is the best course of action.

The **UN Carbon Offset Calculator** shows how flying impacts a household's emissions.

The **ICAO's carbon emissions calculator** allows visitors to analyse the CO2 generated by point-to-point journeys.

Accessible Travel

Public Transport

Philadelphia is working to make its public transit accessible. SEPTA trains, trolleys and buses and PHLASH buses can accommodate wheelchairs and have assistance for visitors with visual or hearing impairments. Side streets and historic avenues can be problematic, with potholes, cobblestones, tree roots, and few audio or visual cues.

Accessible Bars & Clubs

Philadelphia law requires all bars and clubs to be accessible; however, older buildings and historic sites are excluded from this requirement. Still, many venues welcome visitors with accessibility needs to drink, party, dance and make merry.

WEATHER WORRIES

The weather can make Philadelphia's cobblestone streets even trickier to tread on. Rain, snow, slush and ice can make the stones slippery, so watch your step when the weather turns bad.

Wheelchairs

Many museums loan out wheelchairs for visitors who need them. Rent motorized scooters for longer periods of time from scootaround.com, a nationwide organization that can deliver and pick up at your hotel.

The spectacular trove of artworks (mostly impressionist paintings) at the **Barnes Foundation** might seem inaccessible for visitors with visual impairments, but it has a multisensory experience where you can touch replicas of the pieces. The museum also offers audio guides, and the entire space is equipped with smooth floors and elevators, enabling those with mobility difficulties easy access to the galleries. Many of the paintings are at waist or eye level too.

INDEPENDENCE PARK

Many sites in Independence National Historical Park are accessible. American Sign Language interpreters are available with advance notice, and assistive listening devices, touch objects and braille booklets are available at some spots.

Resources

- **phila.gov/departments/mayors-office-for-people-with-disabilities**
The mayor's office has compiled excellent information for people with disabilities about how to enjoy the city.

Nuts & Bolts

Opening Hours

Many restaurants and museums close one day per week (often Monday for restaurants and Tuesday, Wednesday or Thursday for museums). Many eateries close between lunch and dinner.

ATMs 24 hours

Banks 8am–4pm Monday to Friday, to noon Saturday

Bars noon–midnight

Cafes 6am–3pm

Clubs 6pm–2am or later

Grocery stores 8am–8pm

Museums 9am–5pm

Post offices 9am–5pm Monday to Friday, to noon Saturday

Restaurants 6am–11pm

Shops 9am–6pm Monday to Friday, noon–5pm Saturday and Sunday

QUICK INFO

Time zone Eastern (GMT/UTC minus five hours)

Emergency number 911

Population 1.6 million

ELECTRICITY

110-120V/60Hz

Smoking

Smoking is prohibited indoors in all public places, with the exception of a few bars that have been grandfathered in. Cannabis is still illegal to use, though plenty of people do. You will be charged a heavy fine for smoking inside a nonsmoking hotel room, a hotel lobby or a rental car.

Public Holidays

If a holiday falls on a Sunday, the day is observed on the Monday after. Stores might be open on these days, but banks and official government buildings are always closed.

New Year's Day January 1

Martin Luther King Jr Day Second Monday in January

Presidents' Day Third Monday in February

Good Friday Late March or April

Memorial Day Last Monday in May

Juneteenth June 19

Independence Day July 4

Labor Day First Monday in September

Indigenous Peoples' Day Second Monday in October

Veterans Day Second Monday in November

Thanksgiving Day Fourth Thursday in November

Christmas Day December 25

Index

Sights p000 Map pages **p000**

See also separate subindexes for:
Eating p159
Drinking p160
Shopping p161

Eating

Drinking

Shopping

NOTES

Send Us Your Feedback

We love to hear from travelers – your comments help make our books better. We read every word, and we guarantee that your feedback goes straight to the authors. Visit lonelyplanet.com/contact to submit your updates and suggestions.

Note: We may edit, reproduce and incorporate your comments in Lonely Planet products such as guidebooks, websites and digital products, so let us know if you are happy to have your name acknowledged. For a copy of our privacy policy visit lonelyplanet.com/legal.

Acknowledgements

Cover photograph: Benjamin Franklin Bridge (p42). Dylan Sauerwein/Unsplash ©

Back photograph: Liberty Bell (p38). f11photo/Shutterstock ©

THIS BOOK

Destination Editor
Caroline Trefler

Cartographer
Valentina Kremenchutskaya

Production Editor
Megan Graieg

Assisting Editors
Lauren Keith, Aisling O'Sullivan, Maja Vatrić

Book Designer
Dermot Hegarty

Cover Researcher
Marc Backwell

Thanks to
Ronan Abayawickrema, James Appleton, Melanie Dankel, Karen Henderson, Michael Grosberg, Alison Killilea

Published by Lonely Planet Global Limited

CRN 554153

3rd edition – Jan 2025

ISBN 978 1 83758 318 8

10 9 8 7 6 5 4 3 2

Printed in China